IONUMENTAL

ANGER DANS PARIS.

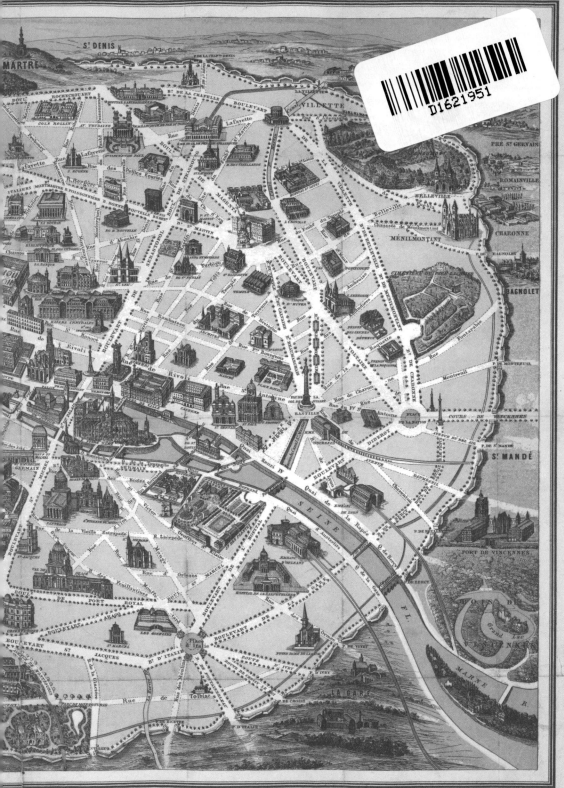

BLOODY
HISTORY
of PARIS

BLOODY HISTORY
of PARIS

Riots, Revolution and Rat Pie

Ben Hubbard

amber
BOOKS

Published by
Amber Books Ltd
74–77 White Lion Street
London
N1 9PF
United Kingdom
www.amberbooks.co.uk
Appstore: itunes.com/apps/amberbooksltd
Facebook: www.facebook.com/amberbooks
Twitter: @amberbooks

ISBN: 978-1-78274-495-5

Editor: Sarah Uttridge
Designer: Jerry Williams
Picture research: Terry Forshaw

Manufactured in China

CONTENTS

INTRODUCTION

In 2015, a new terror struck at the heart of the City of Light. In January, the staff of *Charlie Hebdo* magazine were slaughtered in their offices by Islamic extremists. Ten months later terrorists went on a rampage, mowing down diners with Kalashnikovs and blowing themselves up among their victims at a rock concert.

THE SPILLING OF blood on Parisian streets is nothing new: the city has witnessed centuries of violent rebellion and riot. What had changed was the nature of the threat. The terrorists included homegrown radicals determined to kill in the name of Islam and to avenge past colonial crimes. What deeper challenge could there be to France's core values of liberty, equality and fraternity?

These values were born of the Enlightenment and betrayed by revolutionary terror when the French rose up against their monarch. For centuries, ordinary Parisians had paid with their taxes for their king's life of luxury and decadence. This was famously played out in the vast antechambers of Versailles, a gilded cage constructed by Louis XIV where sexual intrigue and elaborate extravagance were used as a way to keep the nobles under his thumb. Louis ruled in this way for 72 years, but the reign of his successors ended in the revolution of 1789. This introduced the guillotine, or 'national razor', to the world. The policy of purges and bloodshed was introduced with the September massacres, when imprisoned nobles and priests were dismembered and their corpses dragged through the streets.

OPPOSITE: The exhausted conquerors of the Bastille are shown entering the Hôtel de Ville. The 1789 storming of the Bastille was the curtain raiser to the greatest ever Parisian insurrection: the French Revolution.

Habit des Medecins, et autres personnes qui visitent les Pestiferés, Il est de marroquin de leuant, le masque a les yeux de cristal, et un long nez rempli de parfums

ABOVE: An illustration of the protective clothing worn by the so-called 'plague doctors' during a 1348 outbreak of the deadly epidemic.

King Louis XVI was executed for high treason, dispatched one cold, foggy morning in Paris in front of a hushed crowd. As the drums rolled and the blade dropped, many turned away in horror: others surged forward to dip their handkerchiefs in the royal blood; some even tasted it. As many as 2600 were killed in this way; the ground beneath the guillotine was so saturated with blood that officials worried the water supply would be contaminated.

Public executions were an ancient Parisian tradition. In the Middle Ages, where residents had to run a gauntlet of bandits, brothels and boars in the Île de la Cité, capital punishment in public squares was meant as a form of deterrence, but was often treated as entertainment. Prostitutes were stripped to the waist and whipped, thieves had their throats slit, and petty criminals had their faces branded with hot irons. Murderers and rapists were hanged; heretics and sodomites burned at the stake. Suicides would be ritually hanged for their 'offence against God'.

Religious terror permeated every aspect of Parisian society in the Middle Ages. Inquisitors even placed another order of the Church, the crusading Knights Templar, on trial for sodomy, heresy and necromancy. Many confessed to these crimes while having their feet roasted over a fire. But the Templar leader Jacques de Molay retracted his confession while being burned at the stake, placing a curse on Pope Clement and King Philippe le Bel. Within a year, both were dead and Paris was struck by a terrible new affliction: the Black Death.

More than 700 people a day died at the peak of this epidemic, which no one could treat. Doctors dressed in sinister bird-type masks lanced victims' black boils and fed them foul-tasting brews concocted by alchemists. Others, believing the plague to be a divine punishment, rounded up and burned the city's cats, lepers and Jews – all considered apostles of hell.

Religious killing took new forms during the wars between Catholics and Protestants in the 16th century. During the 1572 Saint Bartholomew Massacre, a decrepit hawthorn bush allegedly sprang back to life when Catholics threw hundreds of murdered Protestants into pits. But whether the killing was in the name of religion or politics, or both, the result was the same – a mounting pile of death. During the Terror, rotting corpses and severed heads forced their way to the surface of cemeteries and burst through into nearby basements. The city's Père Lachaise Cemetery itself became a killing ground in 1871, with Paris revolutionaries slaughtered against the Communards' Wall.

A year earlier, bones from cemeteries were exhumed by the starving poor during the Prussian siege and ground up to make flour. Richer Parisians were able to dine on delicacies from the city zoo, including consommé of elephant, bear chops, and antelope terrine. The wrath of the poor finally turned on the rich in the Paris Commune of 1870, which threatened to finish the business started by the 1789 revolution, but instead set the city ablaze.

City sieges and scorched earth policies are familiar motifs in the story of Paris. Henri IV famously burned the fields surrounding Paris and then was left with nothing to eat during his 1590 siege of the city. In the end he converted to Catholicism to win the capital, famously declaring: 'Paris is worth a mass.' In World War I, the fleeing French government told General Joseph-Simon Gallieni to destroy the city rather than let it fall into Prussian hands. Hitler, too, ordered Paris to be annihilated as Parisians took arms against the occupiers. His generals, fortunately, disobeyed, and Paris survived once more.

'Today, the legacy of French colonialism lies deep and wide in Paris.'

The 1944 uprising against the Nazis was a flash of glory during Paris' darkest hours. Thousands had helped round up the city's Jews for deportation to Auschwitz. After the city was liberated and the barricades dismantled, Paris was left to contemplate its long history of anti-Semitism and xenophobia, ancient prejudices that helped spawn new forms of street violence during the Algerian War of Independence.

Today, the legacy of French colonialism lies deep and wide in Paris; the lost and angry children of immigrants in the banlieues (suburbs) have turned readily to terror. Violence in the name of Islam is the ultra-modern form of mass murder in the capital, but insurrection is an old Parisian song. Many thousands have rebelled against the state, the Church and the monarchy during the city's long and bloody history. So the story begins as violently as it ends – with an uprising against the Roman invaders by the people that gave the city its name: the Parisii.

BELOW: Refugees demonstrate against police violence and a lack of adequate shelter in August 2016. Their voices join the many who have protested in Paris over the centuries.

ANCIENT PARIS

The City of Light began as a village of mud and bloodshed. It was built along the quaggy banks of the Seine, a grimy river punctuated by small, habitable islands. One of these was the Île de la Cité, home to the Celtic tribe that gave the city its name: the Parisii.

T HE PARISII HAD been drawn to the Île de la Cité because they believed the Seine to have certain magic qualities that would bring good fortune. Settling in around 250BC, the Parisii prayed to the gods of the river, made offerings of human sacrifice, and understood themselves to be divinely cursed when the corpses bobbed to the surface of the slimy water.

The Seine routinely delivered water-borne diseases and pestilence upstream to the Parisii; it also provided them with a bustling trade route along which their pottery and other handicrafts could be shipped to neighbouring riverbank tribes. The Seine, and river navigation, was therefore an essential part of Parisii life. Little wonder, then, that the first task performed by the invading Romans was to build bridges across the banks of the Île de la Cité. It is also perhaps fitting that the first great conflict of Paris, the city of violent revolution, was a bloody insurrection against the Romans.

The first Roman forays into the region they knew as Gaul began in around 121BC. Then, Roman legions drove deep into the Gaulish heartland to chase

OPPOSITE: The Parisii settlement built on the muddy banks of the Île de la Cité consisted of little more than a series of wooden huts and animal pens.

THE PARISII

The Parisii were one of around 60 Celtic tribes that made up the region described by the Romans as 'Hairy Gaul'. The Romans considered the Gauls uncouth because they wore their hair long, grew moustaches, and were often bare-chested.

The Parisii believed in many gods and held deep-rooted superstitions, such as fearing that the sky might one day fall upon their heads. Strabo, an ancient Greek geographer (c. 64BC–24AD), noted that the Gauls were not only 'war-mad, high-spirited and quick for battle', but also enthusiastic about joining together in defence of a cause, or against a common enemy, a sentiment that has echoed throughout the ages of Parisian history. Strabo elaborates:

'As for their might, it arises partly from their large physique and partly from their numbers. And on account of their trait of simplicity and straightforwardness they easily come together in great numbers, because they always share in the vexation of those of their neighbours whom they think wronged.' (Strabo, *The Geography*, translated by H.L. Jones)

RIGHT: Strabo the Greek noted the Parisii were: 'war-mad, and both high-spirited and quick for battle, although otherwise simple and not ill-mannered.'

marauding Celtic tribes that had been harassing Rome's borders. This policy was updated to include invasion and occupation. In 54BC, the ambitious general and proconsul Julius Caesar marched his armies into Gaul, determined to suck the country dry and put any and all detractors to the sword. Caesar had created a mountain of debt in Rome furthering his political career. The young patrician's generous handouts and lavish gladiatorial games had won him popular affection and acclaim, but he had borrowed heavily against future earnings to meet the cost. Now, Caesar needed not only a king's ransom in war booty, but a Gaulish campaign so successful that any political rival would reconsider standing between him and absolute power. In the end, Caesar would achieve his goals, at least for a time. His campaigns in Gaul were a series of brilliant military victories and heavy civilian casualties – an estimated one million Gauls were killed during Caesar's eight-year campaign.

It was also by Caesar's hand, in his multi-volumed *Commentaries on the Gallic Wars*, that we first hear about the settlement of Paris. Known to the Romans as Lutetia, perhaps derived from *lutum*, the Latin word for mud, the settlement was described by Caesar simply as 'a town of the Parisii, situated on an island in the river Seine.' The Parisii were too small to be a threat to Caesar in his first incursions into the tribal heartland of Gaul in 54BC. After a brief and brutal suppression of any tribe that opposed him, Caesar went to work on those who offered continued resistance.

OPPOSITE: The 486AD Battle of Soissons fought between Syagrius, the last Roman commander of Gaul, and King Clovis I, represented a turning point for Frankish fortunes in France.

The Parisii were of little interest militarily; they were warriors who wielded Iron Age weaponry, but they did not have the muscle to challenge the might of Rome. Instead, Caesar's spies had singled out the tribe as a virtually harmless element that might be of use as collaborators. Caesar saw the logic in this; with friendly allies on the ground he could channel his energies into defeating the large, dangerous tribes that refused to submit, such as the Arverni, Carnutes and Senones.

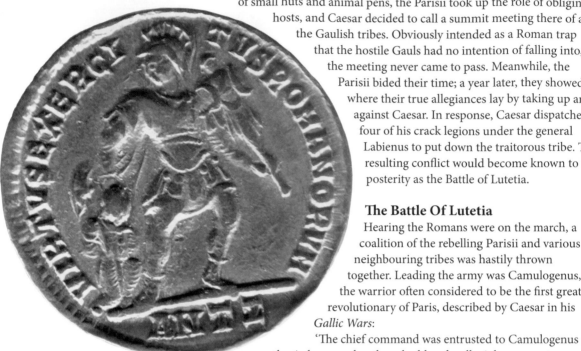

Lutetia also had something of a strategic central position that Caesar could use to his advantage. Although the settlement was nothing more than a grouping of small huts and animal pens, the Parisii took up the role of obliging hosts, and Caesar decided to call a summit meeting there of all the Gaulish tribes. Obviously intended as a Roman trap that the hostile Gauls had no intention of falling into, the meeting never came to pass. Meanwhile, the Parisii bided their time; a year later, they showed where their true allegiances lay by taking up arms against Caesar. In response, Caesar dispatched four of his crack legions under the general Labienus to put down the traitorous tribe. The resulting conflict would become known to posterity as the Battle of Lutetia.

The Battle Of Lutetia

Hearing the Romans were on the march, a coalition of the rebelling Parisii and various neighbouring tribes was hastily thrown together. Leading the army was Camulogenus, the warrior often considered to be the first great revolutionary of Paris, described by Caesar in his *Gallic Wars*:

'The chief command was entrusted to Camulogenus the Aulercan, who, though old and well-nigh worn out, was nevertheless singled out for the distinction because of his exceptional knowledge of warfare. He, noticing a continuous marsh which flowed into the Seine and greatly increased the difficulties of the whole locality, halted there and decided to prevent our troops from crossing.' (Julius Caesar, *Commentaries on the Gallic Wars*, translated by W. McDevitte and W. Bohn)

The marshes Caesar mentions, situated on the Right Bank of the Seine, presented a formidable barrier to Labienus' legionaries, as Camulogenus knew. At first, Labienus ordered his men to fill in the marsh with earth and stones, in an attempt to build a road over it. When this failed, Labienus decided to outflank the Parisii and marched his army south to the nearby settlement of Metiosedum, where he could safely cross the Seine.

Metiosedum was a small island belonging to the Senones, enemies of the Romans whose fighting men were mostly detained in battle against Caesar's army at Gergovia in the south. Labienus ordered his men aboard 50 small fishing boats that were strapped together and launched towards Metiosedum, which was duly laid waste. Labienus then crossed the river and marched his army at full speed to Lutetia, approaching the town from its south side. But, as Labienus' army came into view, Camulogenus set fire to the bridges leading into Lutetia and a large

ABOVE: This gold *solidus* was excavated from the Roman remains on the Île de la Cité and depicts the emperor Julian. One solidus was worth 14 *denarii*, and it became the standard currency of Lutetia during the Late Roman Empire.

OPPOSITE: The first inhabitants of Paris, the Parisii, survived primarily by fishing and trading with other Celtic tribes along the Seine.

part of the settlement itself. Once again thwarted in his attempts to cross onto the island, Labienus retreated from Lutetia and waited for nightfall.

The general's problem was now larger than simply overcoming Camulogenus' forces at Lutetia; reports had reached Labienus that Caesar had been beaten at the Battle of Gergovia and forced to retreat. This had freed up warriors from the Bellovaci tribe, who were now heading towards Labienus at full battle-march.

It was no longer enough for Labienus to provoke Camulogenus into a pitched battle: Lutetia had to be taken, and taken before the Romans became pinned between the Parisii and the approaching Bellovaci.

Caesar describes the dilemma facing Labienus:

'Confronted suddenly with these supreme difficulties, he [Labienus] saw that he must have recourse to personal courage. Towards evening he called together a council of war. Urging them to carry out his commands with care and energy, he

'The resulting conflict would become known to posterity as the Battle of Lutetia.'

Vercingetorix throws down his arms before Caesar after his defeat at the Battle of Alesia. The Gaul would be paraded during Caesar's 46BC triumph in Rome, and then strangled before the crowd.

ABOVE: According to Caesar, Gaulish warriors fought with swords, javelins, bows and arrows, and formed tight phalanxes against Roman cavalry charges. From the first century BC, a core of professional Gaulish soldiers fought alongside freemen.

assigned each of the vessels which he had brought down from Metiosedum to a Roman knight, and ordered them at the end of the first watch to proceed silently four miles downstream and there to await him. He left as garrison for the camp the five cohorts which he regarded as least steady for action; he commanded the remaining five of the same legion to start upstream at midnight with all the baggage, with great uproar. He got together small boats also, and despatched these in the same direction with great noise of oars in the rowing. A short time afterwards he himself marched out silently with three legions, and made for the spot where he had ordered the vessels to put in.' (Julius Caesar, *Commentaries on the Gallic Wars*, translated by W. McDevitte and W. Bohn)

A storm during the night had prevented Camulogenus' scouts from detecting any Roman activity. Then, just before daybreak, reports came in of at least two Roman river crossings by boat. In response, Camulogenus split his army in three, ordering one to stay put, one to march downstream to attack the Roman base, and one to march upstream to where Labienus' diversion was creating a din.

If Camulogenus had not divided his army, it is likely he would have overcome Labienus' legions, which he met in a pitched battle on a plain just west of Lutetia. However, luck was not on Camulogenus' side. Labienus' 7th Legion attacked Camulogenus' facing army on its right flank and quickly broke the line, sending many warriors into flight. The legion was then able to manoeuvre behind Camulogenus' army, which was focused on a frontal attack with the 12th legion, and attack from the rear.

Despite the destruction of the Gaulish line, the warriors refused to surrender and fought to the end. Neither was there any quarter from the Romans; the legionnaires slaughtered the Gauls to a man, Camulogenus among them.

With the battle won, Labienus became the de facto ruler of Lutetia; those of Camulogenus' men not involved in the battle joined the great Gaulish leader Vercingetorix at the final rout of the Gauls at the Battle of Alesia. Among those who fought and lost against the Romans that day were around 8000 Parisii warriors, as recorded by Caesar. Those who survived became part of the Roman Empire; the foundations of the Parisii settlement would be covered by the familiar buildings of a Roman city.

Gallo-Roman Paris

Roman Lutetia never became a grand city to rival the majesty of Rome. However, over 300 or so years of Roman rule it became a prosperous trading centre that enjoyed the peace and political stability of the *Pax Romana*, or 'Roman Peace'.

Like all people conquered by Rome who did not end up in the amphitheatre or slave market, the Parisii were gradually assimilated into the empire. In fact, their integration was so effective that they quelled a local uprising against the Romans in 100AD. Apparently abandoning their propensity for rebellion, the Parisii argued that an uprising would severely damage them in the place that hurt most – their pockets. Revolution, after all, is bad for business.

Most of the time, Paris, and Gaul as a whole, served the franchise known as the Roman Empire. The Gauls paid their taxes, appointed their own nobles as administrators and magistrates, supplied troops when needed, and generally co-operated. In return, the Gauls were free to follow their own traditions, dress as they pleased, and, as long as they offered up the odd piece of incense to the imperial cult, worship their own gods.

Roman Lutetia

The centre of the imperial cult in Lutetia – or Paris, 'the city of the Parisii', as it became known in the fourth century AD – was a basilica in the centre of the Île de la Cité. A road cut through the Isle from north to south and linked it to the larger town on the Left Bank via two bridges. Whereas there were few structures of note on the Right Bank, the Left Bank contained all of the great architectural icons of a Roman city, including three public bath houses, a theatre, an aqueduct and an amphitheatre. The basilica made up the lodgings of the emperor Julian (330–

BELOW: This map of Lutetia was drawn by eighteenth century cartographer Jean-Baptiste Bourguignon d'Anville based on descriptions by Caesar and Strabo. Today, the Île de la Cité remains the central heart of Paris.

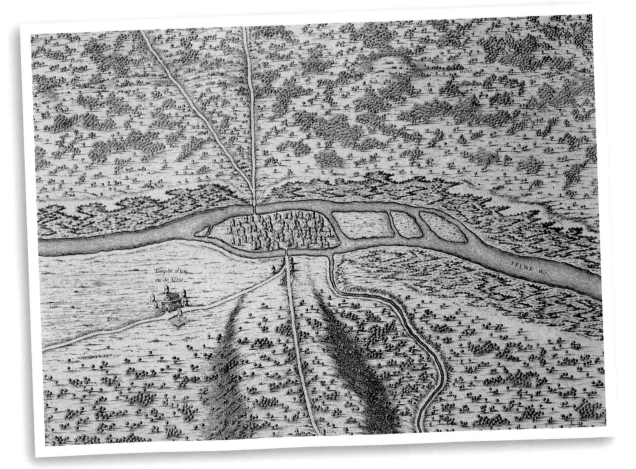

363AD), a man so taken with the city's agreeable climate and abundance of figs and grape vines that he made Paris his de facto home in 358AD rather than lead his legions into the less appealing regions of the unconquered Middle East. Julian was even crowned emperor on the Île de la Cité, a gesture emulated by Napoleon Bonaparte in 1804. Julian even liked the Parisii, despite their obvious savagery, and once likened his position within their relationship as 'like some huntsman who associates with and is entangled among wild beasts. '

Julian's acceptance of the Parisii, despite their apparent vulgarities, was partly to do with their paganism; the Parisii's worship of many gods, after all, was not far removed from that of the Romans. Julian himself was a fervent anti-Christian and even tried to reinstate paganism as the main Roman religion, despite an edict from Emperor Constantine in 313AD that decriminalized Christianity and encouraged its worship. However, despite Constantine's efforts, the persecution of Christians continued throughout the empire into the fifth century, including in Gaul. The amphitheatre in Paris, the Arènes de Lutèce, could accommodate 15,000

THE PARISII CAPITAL

Emperor Julian professed his love for Paris in this extract from his 362AD satire *Misopogon*, or 'beard-hater'. It is also the first known description of Paris:

'I happened to be in winter quarters at my beloved Lutetia for that is how the Celts call the capital of the Parisii. It is a small island lying in the river; a wall entirely surrounds it, and wooden bridges lead to it on both sides. The river seldom rises and falls, but usually is the same depth in the winter as in the summer season… The winter too is rather mild there, perhaps from the warmth of the ocean, which is not more than nine hundred stades distant, and it may be that a slight breeze from the water is wafted so far; for sea water seems to be warmer than fresh. Whether from this or from some other cause obscure to me, the fact is as I say, that those who live in that place have a warmer winter. And

a good kind of vine grows thereabouts, and some persons have even managed to make fig-trees grow by covering them in winter with a sort of garment of wheat straw and with things of that sort, such as are used to protect trees from the harm that is done them by the cold wind.' (Emperor Julian, *Misopogon*, translated by Wilmer Wright)

LEFT: Emperor Julian presides over a religious debate about Christianity, which he despised. He was consequently remembered as 'Julian the Apostate' by the Church.

S ✝ BLA NDINÆ

The torturous martyrdom of Blandina the Gaul is recounted in the *Historia Ecclesiastica* of Eusebius, which reported: 'the heathen themselves admitted that never yet had they known a woman suffer so much or so long.'

ABOVE: Saint Denis, shown here at Notre-Dame Cathedral, was one of the Catholic Church's most famous cephalophores: a saint who had been martyred by beheading. Today, he is venerated as a patron saint of Paris.

OPPOSITE: Protector of Paris, Saint Geneviève here prevents Attila the Hun from entering the city. In reality, Attila came nowhere near Paris and instead decided to chance his luck in the south of France.

spectators for a day of entertainment that included animal hunts, gladiatorial contests, and public executions of Christians. In Rome, these executions had reached new heights of sadism under Emperor Nero, who slaughtered hundreds of Christians at a time in the Colosseum and often devised novel ways of killing them. One of Nero's inventions was the *tunica molesta*, a shirt soaked in pitch that was worn by Christians before they were crucified and set alight. It was even said Nero once lit the grounds of his palace using these macabre human torches.

Arguably the most famous Christian martyr in Gaul was Blandina, a Lyon slave girl who had been arrested with her Christian owner and tortured for so many hours that her exhausted tormentor could go on no longer. Blandina's answer to every question during her torture was famously: 'I am a Christian, and we commit no wrongdoing.' After being condemned to be fed to wild animals, Blandina was tied to a stake in the Lyon amphitheatre, but, according to legend, no beast would touch her, sensing she was a child of God. Finally, Blandina was whipped, laid upon a red-hot iron grate, wrapped in a net, and thrown before a rampaging bull, which tossed her about on its horns. When this did not kill the slave girl, she was stabbed with a dagger, which, finally, made her martyrdom complete.

Paris had its own cherished Christian martyr, who became one of the patron saints of the city: Saint Denis. Although accounts are often muddled, the legend broadly places Denis, a 90-year-old missionary from Italy, in Paris during the middle of the third century. Here, Denis spent his time converting heathens to Christianity and smashing pagan statues, until he was eventually arrested alongside two of his clergy. The three were then imprisoned on the Île de la Cité and sentenced to execution by beheading. On the day of reckoning, the three Christians were marched along the Right Bank to Montmartre where a soldier executed them. However, Denis' decapitated body picked up its head and carried it 10km (6 miles) to the southeast, preaching a sermon as it walked. At the place where the Benedictine abbey of Saint-Denis was founded, Denis finally collapsed, later earning him a posthumous canonization. Denis was dead, but his mark remained, and pagan Lutetia continued its violent journey towards becoming Christian Paris.

The Decline of Rome

Christianity provided a measure of comfort to the Parisii during the dark age that now engulfed Lutetia and most of Europe. By now, the city was a bustling metropolis spreading from the Île de la Cité onto its Left Bank, and boasting an array of churches, gardens and fine civic structures. But the nearby marshlands and forests outside the city walls bristled with bandits and roving barbarians. As the fourth century ended, incursions by Germanic tribes, such as the Goths and

Franks, were reported with alarming frequency. Rome, the great protector of all within her enormous empire, was crumbling.

At the beginning of the fifth century, Paris and Gaul were following Rome into decline. As the empire retreated into its eastern capital of Constantinople, it left Gaul hopelessly exposed. Internally, Gaul's administrative capital in Paris suffered revolts, famine, and a growing absence of any central authority. In 406AD, a large throng of Visigoths streamed across the border of Gaul and began raiding and then occupying the land taken from the Gauls.

'A great Hun Army led by Attila was snaking its way across Europe.'

As the last vestiges of the Gallo-Roman army fought back against the barbarian hordes flowing in from Germany, it seemed impossible that Gaul would be able to defend itself. Worse news was to come: a great Hun army led by Attila was snaking its way across Europe. Attila's barbarity was the stuff of nightmares; during his European campaigns, he had ordered local women to be raped, tortured, and then torn apart by wild horses, their dismembered limbs left for wild dogs to feast on. Now, Attila fixed his gaze on the weak and vulnerable Gaul. In 451AD he crossed the Rhine and headed for Paris, razing local villages and massacring their inhabitants. As streams of homeless refugees made their way to the defensive walls of Paris, the local population also began a mass, panicked exodus from the city. Paris, helpless and alone, had never needed a hero so badly.

BELOW: Saint Geneviève protects a child in the folds of her robes as she looks east from the Pont de la Tournelle. In the child's arms is a ship which symbolizes the city of Paris.

It was then that a most unlikely figure emerged to rally the city. According to legend, Geneviève (419–512AD) was a feverish young orphan who became a nun at 15 after surviving various adversities, and now spoke of her vision that Paris would be saved. She pleaded with the populace not to leave, exclaiming that the Huns would not come and that everyone should kneel and pray. To prove her point, she picked grain outside the city walls, a place where few others dared go.

Whether because of divine inspiration, or Attila's decision to bypass Paris to focus his energies further south, the city was saved. Today, a statue of Geneviève – Paris' patron saint alongside Saint Denis – stands on the Pont de la Tournelle, at the edge of the old fortified city, looking out towards future invaders.

Enter the Franks

Geneviève would continue her role as protector of Paris as well as becoming its chief negotiator during incursions by the Franks, the barbarians who followed Attila. A tribe from Germany, the Franks were a fierce warrior people, many of whom had fought alongside its legionaries as Rome's allies. Now these same Franks were helping the invaders of Rome's crumbling 'Hairy Gaul'. Although the Franks had a reputation for savage and ruthless opportunism, some considered them more reasonable than their barbarian counterparts now streaming out of Germany to spread fire and ruin across Europe.

The Merovingian Franks, in particular, were thought more refined than most and were once described as 'fairly cultivated for a barbarian people' by Agathias, a Greek historian of the late Roman Empire:

'They [The Merovingians] have magistrates in their cities and priests and celebrate the feasts in the same way as we do, and, for a barbarian people, strike me as extremely well-bred and civilized and as practically the same as ourselves except for their uncouth style of dress and peculiar language.'
(Agathias, *The Histories*, translated by J. Frendo)

The Merovingians gained credit from commentators of the day for their adherence to certain Roman traditions; however, it was the Frankish conversion to Christianity that really secured their reputation. From the kingdom of the Franks the Christian nation of France was born. Charles de Gaulle once remarked that: 'For me, the history of France begins with Clovis.' The 'Christian' Franks nevertheless showed an insatiable desire for power, plunder and carnage.

The Merovingians

Geneviève was a pivotal figure in the Frankish takeover. Originally helping to organize Paris against the Frankish invaders, Geneviève later smoothed the way for their annexation of the city and also their later Christianization. The pagan Merovingian king Clovis began this process after being baptized by Geneviève in 496AD; several thousand of his warriors followed suit. While Saint Denis and Geneviève were considered the spiritual founders of France, King Clovis is often believed to be the establisher of its early politics. Simply put, the Frankish government, based at its capital in Paris, was based around a military hierarchal rule that resembled an early form of feudalism: the king and his warriors made up the upper tier of this system, and working people – peasants, blacksmiths, artisans – made up the lower.

The militarized nature of Merovingian society was precisely the reason why Paris, which still retained its Roman garrison town fortifications, held particular appeal as a stronghold for the Franks. On the flat plains outside its city walls, the Merovingians were able to hold their annual meetings, great festivals of force and bravado where grand claims were put forward about future intended targets of conquest. On show among

ABOVE: A depiction of the Frankish migrations into Gaul, part of the European barbarian invasions which began around 300AD.

BELOW: Childebert I was one of Clovis' sons who reigned as king of Paris between 511 and 558AD.

THE FRANCISCA

The Frankish name is thought to have derived from their notorious throwing axe, *the francisca*. With a shaft length of around 40cm (16in) and a bearded blade around 15cm (6in) long, the *francisca* was a brutally effective weapon that concentrated all the energy of the throw into its sharp cutting blade. This gave the axe enough force to cleave several inches into a man's head. Procopius, a sixth-century historian from Palestine, described the Franks and their weaponry:

'They had a small body of cavalry about their leader, and these were the only ones armed with spears, while all the rest were foot soldiers having neither bows nor spears, but each man carried a sword and shield and one axe. Now the iron head of this weapon was thick and exceedingly sharp on both sides, while the wooden handle was very short. And they are accustomed always to throw these axes at a signal in the first charge and thus to shatter the shields of the enemy and kill the men.' (Procopius, *The Wars of Justinian*, translated by H.B. Dewing)

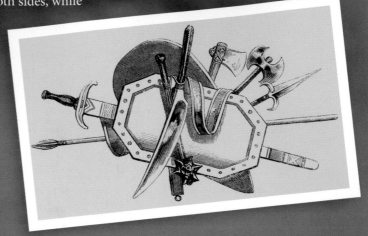

RIGHT: Merovingian armies armed themselves with mail coats, helmets, lances, swords, axes and shields.

the men and weaponry of these events were siege engines based on the Roman design. Clovis, in particular, trod a line between the old traditions of Rome – an empire that he wished to emulate – and the new Christian god. Clovis ruled using Roman tax systems, enacted a Christian framework that involved the Christian priests, and governed as an absolute sovereign, a model that would serve other French leaders well in the centuries to follow.

Clovis on Campaign

Clovis' brutal reign is described in the *History of the Franks*, by the French bishop Gregory of Tours. Gregory recounts the story of a vase plundered from a church in the Gaulish kingdom of Soissons during an early raid by the Franks. A priest from the church appealed to Clovis to return the ecclesiastical relic, but one of his men protested, shouting that all the plunder was to be shared equally and did not belong to one man. With that, the warrior smashed the vase. Aware the crowd was waiting for a violent response, Clovis smiled magnanimously and appeared to accept the warrior's action. However, Clovis later revealed his true nature:

'At the end of a year he ordered all his host to assemble fully equipped at the March parade, to have their arms inspected. After having passed in review all the other warriors, he came to him who had struck the vase. "None," said he, "has brought hither arms so ill-kept as yours; nor lance, nor sword, nor battle-axe are in condition for service." And wresting from him his axe he flung it on the ground. The man stooped down a little to pick it up, and forthwith the King, raising with both hands his own battle-axe, drove it into his skull, saying, "Thus did to the vase of Soissons!" On the death of this fellow he made himself greatly feared.' (Gregory of Tours, *History of the Franks*, translated by Ernest Brehaut)

As Clovis united the various Frankish factions under his rule and consolidated his power base, the king's violence and megalomania deepened. Anyone who seemed to have wronged him was punished or killed. One such was Chararic, a Frankish king who had refused to help Clovis in his war against Syagrius, the last Roman commander of Gaul. Instead Chararic stood aloof, waiting to see who would emerge as victor. It was Clovis, who had Chararic and his son imprisoned and tortured; he then allowed the pair to repent by shaving their heads and becoming priests. But when he heard that Chararic's son had said their hair would grow long again in time, Clovis had them both beheaded and their treasure and territory confiscated.

Ally to Foe

In another episode, Clovis learned that an old ally, King Sigobert of Cologne, was ill. He sent a message to Sigobert's son, Chloderic, that he would remain allied to his kingdom should his father die. It is unclear if Chloderic misinterpreted the message, because, after receiving it, he entered the tent where his father was sleeping and murdered him. He then offered Clovis a chest full of his father's treasure as a good-will gesture. Clovis refused the gift, but sent two messengers to take a closer look at it. They then asked that Chloderic plunge his arms into the chest to show them how deep the treasure went, and when he did so they beheaded him.

Clovis denied any part in the murder. He even travelled from Paris to Cologne to exonerate himself in person, saying: 'It is not for me to shed the blood of one of my fellow kings, for that is a crime...' Clovis then murdered a petty king called Ragnachar, a relative who had also warred with him against Syagrius. The story goes that Ragnachar was notoriously stingy and a hoarder of war booty, which was normally shared out among a king's military commanders. Upon hearing that Ragnachar's commanders were becoming mutinous, Clovis wooed them with gifts of 'gold' amulets and belts, although on closer

BELOW: Despite his bloodthirsty legacy, Clovis also oversaw a crucial period of French cultural and spiritual transformation, as the Western Roman Empire gave way to Germanic kings and their widespread conversion to Christianity.

OPPOSITE: Clovis' victory over Roman commander Syagrius at the Battle of Soissons is widely considered to mark the end of Western Roman rule outside Italy. Syagrius fled the battlefield and was later stabbed to death.

inspection these turned out to be bronze. However, this was enough to fatally divide Ragnachar's army and enable Clovis to declare war on the king and win.

Ragnachar and his brother Ricchar were both captured while trying to flee the battlefield following their defeat, and were brought before Clovis with their hands bound. Clovis asked Ragnachar: 'Why have you humiliated our family in permitting yourself to be bound? It would have been better for you to die.' He then split Ragnachar's skull with his axe and turned to Ricchar, saying: 'If you had aided your brother, he would not have been bound', before ending his life in the same manner.

After killing a further relative, Clovis was heard complaining that there was no one left to succeed him. However, after Clovis' death in 511AD, his four sons divided Frankia between them. They ruled with their father's duplicity and violence, a tradition that continued for nearly 200 years until the Merovingian Franks were replaced by the Carolingian dynasty.

One of the better parts of Clovis' legacy was the development of religious buildings in Paris. Relics of Saint Vincent had been interred in a shrine on the Left Bank, in today's Saint-Germain-des Prés, the burial site of many of the Frankish kings. On the Right Bank, the church of Saint-Martin-des-Champs was erected where a miracle had been performed on a leper. A cathedral to Saint-Étienne was constructed on the Île de la Cité, alongside six other churches that had sprung up by the eighth century. However, by the time Charles Martel of the Carolingian dynasty became king, the power of Paris was on the wane.

BELOW: By smiting down the soldier who had smashed the vase of Soissons, Clovis showed himself to be vengeful and also sympathetic to the Christians. Both were valuable lessons to be learned by his men.

darmes et habillemens de guerre
le ledit clouis se part et polla
rite de loillons et fureut de lou
pettes au deuant de ladite plaine

Et finablement par lorce de proelle et vaillant
conquilt et milt a lon obeillance icelle riue
et en crpulla hors louages capitaine dudit
lieu qui eltoit filz de gillon le Roumain

Unlike their predecessor, Clovis, the Carolingians did not always use Paris as their capital. Instead, a policy of almost incessant warfare meant the Carolingians kept their capital in different cities, depending on which held the most strategic position at the time. Paris, however, was of great interest to the hordes of Saracens menacing the Gaulish borders to the south. By raiding the churches of Paris, Charles Martel was able to raise an army large enough to stop the Saracens reaching the city, and the Parisians were temporarily spared another invasion.

'In truth, the city and the emperor had little to do with each other.'

The most famous of the Carolingians was Charlemagne, crowned Holy Roman Emperor in 800 by Pope Leo III. Charlemagne was a short, fat man who bore little resemblance to the statue erected to him outside today's Notre Dame Cathedral. In truth, the city and the emperor had little to do with each other. Charlemagne ruled his empire from Aix-la-Chapelle, and Paris seemed all but forgotten by its emperor. The city was overlooked once more under Charlemagne's son Louis the Pious and his grandsons, who divided the empire between them.

BELOW: Here, Charlemagne, king of the Franks, is crowned Holy Roman Emperor. This made Charlemagne the first recognized emperor in Western Europe since the fall of the Western Roman Empire more than 300 years earlier.

However, the city was attracting a new peril in the north. From the end of the eighth century, the sea raiders known as the Vikings were raiding monasteries along the English coastline. Reports of their atrocities, including the wanton slaughter of monks, enslavement of local villagers and the robbery of ecclesiastical treasure, soon reached the ears of the priests and parishioners of Paris. In the new century, the heathen Norsemen were soon heading towards Christian Frankia.

FRANKISH CRIME AND PUNISHMENT

Salic Law was the code of the Franks, based on old Germanic law and compiled by Clovis in around 500AD. The code excluded women from inheriting property or succeeding to the throne. It also decreed that kingdoms be split up among all of the surviving male heirs, a law which caused centuries of bloodshed in France over the succession. Salic Law also provided detailed punishments for many criminal acts, from small misdemeanours to physical injury and murder. Compensation payments were made in Roman *solidi*.

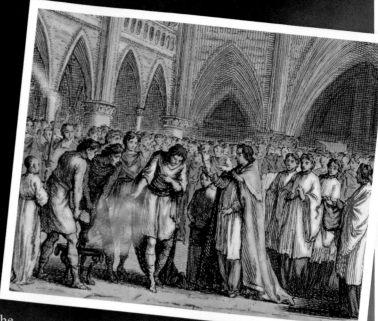

At the lesser end of the scale the code recommends: 'He who claims that someone else is covered in dung shall be liable to pay three *solidi*.' And, 'A man who accuses another of throwing down his shield in battle and fleeing, without being able to prove it, should pay three *solidi*.' Further punishments were suggested for wounds, both inflicted and attempted:

'He who maims another man's hand or foot, or gouges or strikes out his eye, or cuts off his ear or nose shall be liable for 100 *solidi*.'

'He who strikes another man on the head so that the brain shows, and it is proved against him, shall be liable to pay 15 *solidi*.'

'He who castrates a freeman or cuts into his penis so that he is incapacitated shall be liable to pay 100 *solidi*… But if he takes the penis away entirely he shall be liable to pay 200 *solidi* in addition to nine *solidi* for the doctor.' (*The Salic Law*, translated by Ernest F. Henderson)

ABOVE: Trial by ordeal was practiced by the Catholic Church up until the thirteenth century.

Punishment for non-payments included the removal of an eye, nose or ear. Torture and floggings were common punishments for theft. Those accused of a crime would sometimes be given the choice of a trial by ordeal to prove their innocence. This would typically include the accused dipping their hand into a pot of boiling water to retrieve a stone. The depth of the water would be determined by the numbers of accusations: up to the wrist for one accusation; and up to the elbow for three. The ordeal would be conducted in a church, with the attendees required to pray that God would reveal the truth. The hand would then be bound for three days and reexamined. If there was no evidence of wounds from the scalding, it was assumed the accused had been healed by God and was therefore innocent.

THE MIDDLE AGES

In 845, the worst fears of the people of Paris were realized. In March, a great Viking army aboard 120 longships sailed up the Seine towards the city. The brutality and bloodshed that followed would shake the foundations of French Christendom and plunge Paris into a violent new epoch.

REMOTE MONASTERIES AND churches were typical targets for Viking raiders, who would plunder ecclesiastical treasure and condemn those not slaughtered into slavery. But now, it seemed the heathen warriors had something more ambitious in mind. As the Viking longships approached Paris, a monk from the monastery of Saint-Germain-des-Prés recorded the terror: 'In the year of our Lord 845, the vast army of Northmen breached the frontiers of the Christians. This was something that we never heard or read of happening before.'

Standing between the 5000-strong Viking force and Paris, the centre of which still lay on the fortified Île de la Cité, was the Frankish King Charles the Bald. Charles had learned that the Vikings had raided Rouen on their way to Paris, and he was determined not to let the heart of Frankish Christendom be similarly undone. He split his army into two parts, one for each side of the Seine, and resolved that the heathen fleet should not pass. Dividing his force, however, was a costly error. The Vikings easily overcame half of Charles' army on one side of the river, while the other half looked on helplessly. To honour their god Odin and

OPPOSITE: The Knights Templar were among those persecuted by the tyrant king, Philippe le Bel. After torture by the Inquisition, members of the crusading order were burned at the stake on charges of sodomy, heresy and necromancy.

CUM SEDEAT KAROLUS MAGNO COORONATUS HONORI
EST IOSIAE SIMILIS   PARQUE THEODOSIO

strike terror into those left of Charles' men, the Vikings took 111 men prisoner and hanged them on a small uninhabited island in the Seine.

Now, unmolested by Charles' army, the Vikings quickly landed their ships at the Île de la Cité and fell mercilessly on all who had remained in the city. The monks had led a mass exodus, but many had ignored the order and stayed. The resulting mayhem was typical of a Viking raid on any Christian settlement, although the brutality of the Vikings' violence in Frankia was reported to be particularly barbaric. After indiscriminately slaughtering all the people they could find and plundering any remaining gold and silver, the Vikings relaxed.

The sacking of Paris had revealed troubling news about the man leading the Vikings, a notorious raider of Frankish settlements called Ragnar. This Ragnar is believed by some historians to be the legendary Ragnar Lodbrok, aka 'Ragnar Hairy-Breeks', so named for the impenetrable hair-covered trousers that slowed his demise in a custom-made East Anglian viper pit. A hero of the Icelandic sagas, Ragnar Lodbrok seems to have begun his fighting career with campaigns against Charlemagne the Great, protector of the Franks and Holy Roman Emperor.

ABOVE: After having his breeches removed, Ragnar's saga reports he died in the viper pit with 'snakes hanging off him on all sides.'

OPPOSITE: Grandson to Charlemagne, Charles the Bald did little to prevent the Vikings repeatedly sacking Paris. His nickname was ironic: in reality, Charles was an extremely hirsute man.

Charlemagne had held together his unwieldy empire against ambitious Scandinavian warlords, such as King Godfred of Denmark, through a policy of deliberate aggression. The two had clashed over the small trading settlement of Frisia, today a part of Germany and the Netherlands, which was then an important buffer between the two kingdoms. In a moment of brilliance and bravado Godfred had invaded Frisia and astonished its current occupier, Charlemagne. To make Godfred go away, Charlemagne paid him a ransom of 200 pounds of silver. This was the start of a tradition that became known in England as a Danegeld, a payment made to Viking raiders to cease hostilities and return occupied territory. By 814, both Charlemagne and Godfred were dead; however, in securing the Danegeld from Charlemagne, Godfred had paved the way for the next generation of Viking raiders.

Ragnar, whether the legendary Lodbrok or not, was one of the Viking raiders previously paid off by Charles the Bald, Charlemagne's grandson, with a parcel of land in Frisia. But Charles had later reneged on the deal and the land had been lost. Paris was Ragnar's revenge, and Charles had little choice but to pay the Viking to give the city back to him. This time, the price of the Danegeld was 7000 pounds of silver, in addition to whatever treasure or slaves they could take with them. To add further insult to the people of Frankia, Charles himself suggested that there were other towns further along the river from which Ragnar might profit. Needing no second invitation, Ragnar devastated the villages he passed en route back to Scandinavia. However, the Vikings did not escape unscathed. An epidemic swept through the ships of the Viking fleet, wiping out the majority of the warriors as they returned home. Ragnar survived the epidemic, but feared a divine punishment had been inflicted. King Horik of Denmark, who had financed the Paris raid, offered to release the Parisian prisoners and return the plundered treasure, also suspecting that God was demanding retribution. However, none of this pushed back the Viking tide: Charles' Danegeld had simply bought the Frankish king some

BELOW: Charlemagne watches in dismay over a Viking raid. As Holy Roman Emperor, Charlemagne recognized the relevance of the Viking threat, but was unable to hold back their attacks on his unwieldy empire.

time, and soon a new Viking force would set sail for Paris.

As Frankish monasteries, villages, towns and cities fell before the Viking onslaught, Charles the Bald passed royal edicts banning under penalty of death the sale of horses and weapons to the Norsemen. However, this did not stop the raiders growing rich from slaves, ransom, loot and the Danegeld. Paris, replete with churches and ecclesiastical treasure, became a highly desirable target, as the monk Abbo Cernuus of Saint-Germain-des-Prés described:

'Paris! There you sit in the middle of the Seine, in the midst of the rich lands of the Franks, calling out: I am a city above all others, sparkling like a Queen above them all. All know you by the splendour of your bearing. Whoever lusts after the wealth of France is paying you homage.' (Abbo Cernuus, *Wars of the City of Paris*, translated by Nirmal Dass)

After the humiliation wrought upon Paris by Ragnar in 845, the next Viking to attack the city was his son, Björn Ironside. In 857, Ironside confidently sailed up the Seine and sacked Paris as part of a four-year raiding tour that took him and his fleet into the Mediterranean. Ironside ended up mistakenly sacking the city of Luna, Italy, believing it was Rome, before sailing back to Scandinavia. In Paris, Ironside almost destroyed the city, leaving only four of the city's churches standing.

In 860 came yet another Viking attack. Desperate to protect Paris, Charles the Bald mobilized a large section of the male population to build towers and walls around the Île de la Cité and fortified bridges across the Seine. Charles' theory was that if the Seine were blocked, the Vikings would lose their main thoroughfare to Paris and also further inland. He did not live long enough to see whether his fortifications worked. Instead it was his successor, Charles the Fat, and the protector of Paris, Count Odo, who would bear witness to the largest Viking attack to take place on Frankish soil.

The 885 Siege of Paris

The Viking force, led by the warriors Sigfred and Sinric, was no mere raiding party chancing its luck. Rather, it was a formidable army of thousands of warriors aboard 300 longships. If the newly fortified Paris, complete with two low-lying, longship-blocking bridges, was a surprise to the Viking fleet it did not appear to dampen their determination. When the Viking demands for a Danegeld and safe passage past Paris were denied by Count Odo, the invaders laid siege.

> **'The Viking force was no mere raiding party chancing its luck.'**

If Sigfred and Sinric were expecting Paris to be a walkover, they were wrong. Despite attacking with a variety of siege engines, including towers, battering rams and catapults, the 200-strong Frankish force inside the city walls held strong. For two months the siege continued, with the Vikings filling the Seine with debris and the dead bodies of prisoners, but to no avail.

The Vikings changed tactics, trying to bring down one of the bridges with flaming arrows, stone missiles, and three of their own ships set on fire. The bridge was badly damaged, but still standing. In February, however, heavy rain and gushing river debris swept the bridge off its foundations, giving the Vikings access to one of the city's towers. All inside were quickly killed. However, the integrity of the rest of the Île de la Cité's defences held strong.

CYCLES OF VIOLENCE

From the mid-ninth century, the frequency of Viking raids grew at an alarming rate. Before long, nowhere on Frankish soil could be considered safe. In his *History of the Miracles and Translations of Saint Philibert*, the Frankish monk Ermentarius records the horrors of Viking invasion:

'The number of ships increases, the endless flood of Vikings never ceases to grow bigger. Everywhere Christ's people are the victims of massacre, burning, and plunder. The Vikings over-run all that lies before them, and none can withstand them. They seize Bordeaux, Perigueux, Limoges, Angouleme, Toulouse; they make deserts of Angers, Tours and Orleans. Ships past counting voyage up the Seine, and throughout the entire region evil grows strong. Rouen is laid waste, looted and burnt: Paris, Beauvais, Meaux are taken, Melun's stronghold is razed to the ground, Chartres occupied, Evreux and Bayeux looted, and every town invested.' (Ermentarius, *History of the Miracles and Translations of Saint Philibert*, translated by R. Poupardin)

ABOVE: The 885 Siege of Paris symbolized more than another hit-and-run raid on a Western European settlement: it was a trial of power between Viking and Frank.

After demanding a Danegeld of 60 pounds of silver and being refused by Odo, Sigfred quit the siege and was replaced by another Viking, Rollo. Meanwhile, Odo slipped secretly from the city to plead with Charles the Fat to send reinforcements. Charles was a cowardly leader who had no stomach for a fight with the Norsemen: he was persuaded, however, by Odo's argument that letting Paris fall was tantamount to surrendering Frankia to the enemy. Charles marched his army to Paris, but, rather than attack the besieging Viking force, he set up camp on the nearby Montmartre hill. From here, Charles began negotiations, encouraging the Norsemen to move on and attack nearby Burgundy. Burgundy was in revolt against Charles at the time, and he told the Vikings that it could be easily plundered. He paid Rollo 700 pounds of silver to leave France altogether, a hefty Danegeld that was too good to pass up after the bitter months besieging Paris.

Charles, however, would not dismantle his defensive bridges and Rollo's fleet had to make its way down the Seine by portaging their boats – lifting them out of the river and pulling them across land – along large stretches of the river.

Paris had once again paid for a temporary reprieve, but, in 911, Rollo was back with a new force. This time a new king, Charles the Simple, wasted no time in proposing a deal: a gift of land, a title, and his daughter Gisela's hand in marriage. The stipulation was that Rollo would protect his domain of Normandy and convert to Christianity.

Rollo accepted, married Gisela, and was baptized as Robert I. According to legend, Rollo refused to kiss the foot of Charles the Simple as a symbol of his loyalty and instead had one of his warriors do it for him. Famously, the king was unbalanced during this awkward gesture and fell to the ground.

The Christianization of Rollo and the founding of Normandy symbolized the end of Viking activity in the kingdom of the Franks. The last reported payment of a Danegeld to the Vikings was by King Rudolf in 926; after that, the record books fall silent. Rollo's descendant, however, known to history as William the Conqueror, would show the world in 1066 that Viking raiding blood still ran strongly through Norman veins.

BELOW: Although assembling an army large enough to defeat the Vikings, Charles the Fat instead paid them to go away in peace. Charles also encouraged the Vikings to harry Burgundy, where his subjects were rebelling.

Dawn of the Middle Ages

Medieval Paris still stands in the modern city. It is evident in the grand stone and stained glass of Notre-Dame and Sainte-Chapelle, and the bustling cobbled pavements of the Latin Quarter (so-called for the common language shared by the students who studied there). This Parisian period is often viewed in a rose-coloured light that focuses softly on chivalric kings and graceful queens, knights in white armour, chaste maidens and courtly love.

It is a vision that had nothing to do with the reality of Paris in the new millennium. Instead, the dawn of the Middle Ages broke on a filthy, broken city, left in ruins by murderous Norsemen and given over to degeneracy and vice. The streets below the dilapidated buildings of the Île de la Cité – the city's great stronghold against the Norse invaders – were a festering cesspit of brigands and brothels. Citizens had to navigate a daily gauntlet of bandits and wild pigs running free through the narrow streets. In the small public squares, criminals suffered the punishments of Carolingian law: prostitutes were stripped to their waists and whipped; thieves had their throats slit.

The dynasty ruling France in the eleventh century were the Capetians, who, in a well-worn tradition adopted from the Merovingians, seemed utterly uninterested in Paris. Instead, after basing their capital at Orleans, the Capetians left the rebuilding and repopulation of Paris following the Viking devastation to the Church. The Church at this time was beginning to become a serious force in French politics: it had land, money, and importantly, the support of the Pope in Rome.

The Left Bank, which had been all but abandoned during the time of the Viking peril, was the first focus of the Church's redevelopment plans. It certainly needed a facelift, consisting of little more than fallen wooden fortifications, wild livestock, and filth-caked streets that had turned into goat tracks. The church began its building works with housing for the peasants who served the monks at the Abbey of Saint-Germain-des-Prés. Soon markets, artisans and centres of learning sprang up, and the Left Bank developed a young, vibrant, academic atmosphere.

A great boon to the intellectual rebirth of the Le Bank was the arrival of Peter Abelard, the anti-clerical founder of the university that would later become the Sorbonne. However, Alebard is better known as the castrated lover from the legend of Abelard and Héloïse, a love story still celebrated in Paris for its romantic fatalism and visceral brutality.

ABOVE: To become the Duke of Normandy, Rollo renounced his heretic gods and converted to Christianity. The great invader of England, William the Conquer was a descendant of Rollo's.

OPPOSITE: Refusing to kiss the foot of Charles the Simple, Rollo instead ordered one of his warriors do it for him. The warrior famously toppled the king in the process, to the great merriment of the attending Vikings. Thus, the Duchy of Normandy was born.

ROYAL DISGUST

Anne of Kiev became the wife of Capetian king Henry I (1008–1060), after Henry failed to find a royal fiancé closer to home and sent envoys to search the furthest reaches of Europe. Anne, to the astonishment of the nearly illiterate Henry, could speak five languages and had learned French on her journey to her betrothed in Paris. She was unimpressed with the 'unwashed' French and complained that only three courses were served at her wedding as opposed to the traditional Ukrainian five. She was particularly offended by Paris, of which she wrote in a letter to her father: 'the houses are gloomy, the churches ugly, and the customs revolting.'

RIGHT: Anne of Kiev was shocked by the squalor of Paris and considered her husband an uneducated boor. He loved her passionately.

As the Church consolidated its hold on Paris, it also offered to help the king unite the country. France at the time was a patchwork of independent vassal states, each with an imposing castle at its centre ruled by a lord. This was the result of Clovis' Salic law, which divided a noble's estate between his surviving sons upon his death. The law of inheritance bred strife and warfare through the generations. Violence between the states was commonplace, as was fighting on the streets of Paris. To limit the bloodshed, the Church instituted a 'Truce of God'. This outlawed fighting at any time between monks, women and priests, and prohibited general fighting between Wednesday and Monday, but sanctioned violence at all other times of the week. The Church attempted to unite the feuding lords in crusades designed to battle infidels and claim back the holy land for God.

'By the thirteenth century, Paris had become a city of contradictions.'

The crusades became infamous for the slaughter of heretics. One of the most notorious massacres took place on French territory at Béziers, which was stormed after the town elders refused to hand over those guilty of heresy. When the abbot who led the attacking crusaders was asked how to tell Béziers' Catholics from its heretics, he replied: 'Kill them all for the Lord knoweth them that are His'. Some 20,000 were slaughtered and the town razed.

French kings were careful about which crusades they joined. Often, crusades were most beneficial for kings who stayed at home; they usually bankrupted or killed the lords of powerful vassal states, while also strengthening the emerging trading class. These craftsmen, artisans and blacksmiths often worked as suppliers to crusading knights and were a great boon to local economies, not least in Paris.

One king who preferred to refrain from crusades was the Capetian Philippe Auguste. Philippe avoided a 1209 crusade against the Cathars by explaining to Pope Innocent III that he had too many problems on the domestic front to risk leaving the country. Philippe then spent his energy transforming France from a small feudal state into a large, prosperous kingdom that he ruled from Paris.

Philippe was one of the first French rulers since the Roman emperor Julian to genuinely love the city. He built a fortified wall around its perimeter, gave the Sorbonne its royal charter, continued the building of Notre Dame, and paved the city streets. This last improvement brought a dramatic change to daily Parisian life. Previously, on rainy days the raw sewage thrown into the street had mingled horribly with the mud and dirt that made up the street itself, bringing about an unthinkable stench.

By the thirteenth century, Paris had become a city of contradictions. Under its new king Louis IX, France and Paris prospered: magnificent building works were carried out in the capital, such as Sainte-Chapelle on the Île de la Cité. A new urban class, the bourgeoisie, also played their part in gentrifying the city, which now boasted a burgeoning population of 100,000 people. But despite Paris' new splendour, actually walking around the City of Light was a chancy undertaking.

Philippe The Fair

If murder, thievery, fighting, drunkenness and fornication were commonplace activities on the streets of medieval Paris, so too were the gruesome punishments doled out to the criminals who committed them. By the

BELOW: The Abbey of Saint-Germain-des-Prés was founded by Childebert I in the sixth century and built on the Left Bank so he could see it from his Île de la Cité palace.

Constructed by Louis IX as a shrine to house the holy Crown of Thorns, Sainte-Chapelle has one of the largest collections of stained glass in the world. Its windows were removed in World War II as the Germans advanced on Paris.

OFFICE OF THE PRÉVÔT

An early police force had been set up under Philippe Auguste in the twelfth century in an attempt to curb the city's lawlessness. The officers were called *ribauds*, a word used to describe certain crusaders who had signed up specifically to rape and plunder. The head of the police force later became the *grand prévôt*, or 'provost marshal', a post that was often linked to the criminal underworld. Several *prévôts* were hanged for abuse of power, some of them for the unsanctioned murders of 'guilty' people. The *prévôt* Guillaume de Tignonville (d. 1414), in particular, is remembered for torturing and hanging two university clerics, only for the sentence to be successfully appealed against and overturned. Guillaume was ordered to take down the corpses of the clerics, which had been rotting on a gibbet for several months, and give them a proper burial. No action was taken against the *prévôt* himself, however.

BELOW: Philippe was a stern, physically striking king who believed himself called upon by God to safeguard the moral and spiritual welfare of his subjects. To achieve this, torture and murder were routinely employed.

time Philippe IV took the throne in 1284, public executions had become a commonplace form of entertainment enjoyed by large crowds. Thieves and murderers were usually simply hanged, but others had their eyes torn out, or their faces branded with red-hot irons.

For many Parisians, the greatest villain of all was their king, Philippe IV, otherwise known as Philippe le Bel, 'The Fair', for his pretty looks and icy demeanour. Philippe was a vain, reckless man who encouraged cruelty and came close to bankrupting the country through his financial incompetence. Under Philippe, the political institutions of France were consolidated into three categories: the Nobility, the Clergy, and the Third Estate – the non-privileged class. Representatives from each would meet separately, thereby preventing any semblance of a democracy until the social and political crisis of 1789. Under Philippe, the running of the country cost nearly seven times more than under Philippe Auguste a century earlier. Some of the money was spent on spectacular new buildings – Philippe drew up grandiose plans to rebuild Philippe Auguste's Palais de la Cité into the 'most beautiful place ever seen in France'. To refill his dwindling coffers Philippe enacted new taxes, including those 'for the defence of the realm', confiscated the lands and treasures of rich landowners, and stoked inflation by debasing the currency. He ordered all Jews to be removed from France for the crime of usury and seized their assets; some were burned at the stake as a warning against future resistance.

Next Philippe turned his attention to the Knights Templar, the crusading order that had built its lavish enclave just outside Paris' city walls. The Knights were enormously wealthy

Under Philippe le Bel, many were executed by being burned alive. Hangings, whippings and punishments such as the removal of eyes were also commonplace public events attended by a crowd.

with loot from foreign crusades, a fortune they had multiplied by becoming international moneylenders. They were resented in French society, not just because of their vast riches and ostentatious Parisian dwelling, but also because it was rumoured that they openly practised sodomy.

It was the charges of sodomy, heresy and necromancy, among others, that Philippe brought against the Templars in 1307. He said of their crimes:

'A deplorable and most lamentable matter, full of bitterness and grief, a monstrous business, a thing that one cannot think on without affright, cannot hear without horror, transgressions unheard of, enormities and atrocities contrary to every sentiment of humanity have reached our ears.' (Philippe IV, *The History of the Knights Templars*, Charles Addison)

Philippe said it was right that the land and assets of the Templars be seized pending the outcome of an investigation by the dreaded papal Inquisition. Torture was to be used to extract confessions from the Templars if necessary:

'Before proceeding with the inquiry you are to inform them [the Templars] that the pope and ourselves have been convinced, by their irreproachable testimony of the errors and abominations which accompany their vows and profession: you are to promise them pardon and favour if they confess the

BELOW: As Templar leader Jacques de Molay burned alive, he retracted the confession obtained during his torture and laid a curse upon Philippe, Pope Clement and their offspring.

THE GIBBET OF MONTFAUCON

First built in the thirteenth century, the Gibbet of Montfaucon was a multi-chambered wooden scaffold where prisoners could be hanged or have their bodies displayed as a warning to criminals. Situated near today's Buttes-Chaumont Park, the gibbet was 10m (33ft) high, contained 16 columns and could accommodate dozens of bodies at a time. Corpses were sometimes left in the gibbet for up to three years, making the site notorious for flocks of crows and, during bleak winters, wolves looking to scavenge leftovers. The wooden scaffold was later rebuilt in stone and described by seventeenth-century travel writer Thomas Coryat as 'the fayrest gallowes that I ever saw, built on a little hilocke… with fourteen pillars of free stone.' The gibbet was in use until 1629, and then dismantled in 1760.

RIGHT: The Gibbet of Montfaucon was erected on a hill near today's Place du Colonel Fabien, which lay outside the city walls of Paris during the Middle Ages.

truth, but if not you are to acquaint them that they will be condemned to death.' (Philippe IV, *The History of the Knights Templars*, Charles Addison)

Then, one night, the terror began. The Inquisition stormed the Templar palace, arrested all of the knights there, and confiscated all that they owned. Soon afterwards the public torture of the Templars started. This included fastening the legs of an accused knight in an iron frame, smearing their feet in butter, and roasting them over an open fire. The torturer would be on hand with a bellows to keep the flames high. Most lost the use of their feet in this way; others were reportedly driven mad. Thirty-six Templars died while under interrogation of torture.

The very specific confessions that the Inquisition wished to extract included worshipping a cat, spitting on the cross, and roasting infant children. Confessions often did come at various points during the torture, although at other times they were retracted just before the point of death. This most notably occurred during an episode when 138 Templars were burned at the stake, with several crying out before they succumbed to the flames that their confessions had been false.

te de neuers et de la fille au roy fu fait a paris.
De la meute des pastoureaux.

N cest an comença en france vne
meute sans dilacion. car auca

The leader of the Templars, Jacques de Molay, cursed both Pope Clement and Philippe during his immolation, calling on God to strike down their accomplices and destroy their offspring. Only a month later, Clement was dead from bowel cancer; Philippe himself was killed in a hunting accident later that year. De Molay's curse was often said to have had far more severe consequences than only these two deaths.

Before Philippe perished he indulged in a last piece of barbarity that both shocked and titillated the population of Paris. Opposite the Louvre on the Left Bank, Philippe had built palatial apartments for three of his sons, Louis, Philippe and Charles, and their wives, Marguerite, Jeanne and Blanche. However, Marguerite and Blanche were caught using the residences to meet their lovers, the d'Aulnay brothers, and these two were soon on trial for adultery.

Philippe gave no quarter in his sentence: the d'Aulnays were tortured and skinned alive in front of a cheering crowd before being castrated and disembowelled and their remains hung in a gibbet. Marguerite and Blanche had their heads shaved, a tradition that would also be used on French collaborators after World War II, and were thrown into solitary confinement. Marguerite was later suffocated to death between two mattresses by her husband Louis; Blanche was allowed to live out her days in a convent.

BELOW: Louis X, known as 'Louis the Stubborn', was an unnoteworthy king who reigned during a troubled period of war, hunger and disease.

Curse of the Templars

Parisians naturally assumed that Philippe's early demise was directly related to the curse Jacques de Molay made as he was burned alive. The highly superstitious ancient Parisii had spiritual descendants among the Medieval Parisians. A curse was certainly not something to be scorned or scoffed at. Philippe's death all but sealed the end of the Capetian dynasty that had ruled France for more than three centuries. His three sons held the throne for only 14 years between them, an untimely end befalling each in turn.

De Molay's curse, however, appeared to have wider ramifications for Paris than just the royal succession. The city entered a centuries-long period of strife and ruination that would destroy many of its people. The trouble began in 1314, the year of Philippe's death, when the Great Famine struck France and its capital. Lasting three years, the famine had been brought about by several bad winters that had wiped out harvests and created food shortages everywhere. Urban centres such as Paris were hit hardest; food became scarce and prices skyrocketed.

In place of food and fresh produce, the so-called Pastoureaux, a hodge-podge of disaffected shepherds, unfrocked priests, unemployed peasants, and

OPPOSITE: In 1320, a group of disgruntled subjects known as the Pastoureaux attacked Paris, sacked several of its buildings, and murdered many of the city's Jews.

ABOVE: Here, a plague doctor attempts to treat the disease by lancing a victim's boils. The Black Death held Paris in its grip for over a year and reduced the population by half.

various charlatans, swarmed into Paris. Blaming the famine on the king's inability to launch crusades, the Pastoureaux sacked the city, attacked the *prévôt*, and ransacked the Abbey of Saint-Germain-des-Prés. The mob then rounded up the city's Jews and burned many to death on the Île de la Cité.

King Louis X, son of Philippe and murderer of his wife Marguerite, emptied the city's prisons, apparently to atone for his sins. Predictably, the crime rate spiraled out of control; the streets of Paris ran red. In response to the crime wave sweeping the city, the Gibbet of Montfaucon worked overtime.

Louis X's disastrous reign lasted only two years, bringing a final end to the Capetian line. Isabella, Louis X's sister, was the last surviving child of Philippe, but the Salic law instigated by Clovis forbade female heirs from taking the throne. King Edward III of England was Philippe's grandson and rightful heir, but allowing an Englishman onto the French throne was unthinkable. Instead, the crown went to Philippe's nephew, Philippe de Valois, the first of a new French dynasty. Despite Edward paying homage to Philippe, relations soured after Philippe confiscated his Duchy of Aquitaine, fearing Edward was plotting against him. Edward then challenged Philippe's right to the throne, and the Hundred Years' War began.

Ever since William the Conqueror had invaded England in 1066, English kings had retained some possessions in France, and this was the root cause of the war. Because Edward had support from vassals around France, it also made the conflict something of a civil war. Lasting from 1337, when Edward decided to begin calling himself King of France, to 1453, when England lost the last of its French territories, the Hundred Years' War was an intermittent but seemingly interminable war that placed a great strain on everyday life in Paris.

The most obvious immediate effect of the war was vast numbers of refugees flocking to Paris to escape the atrocities of the English army. In response, Parisians, angered that once again the city was stretched to breaking point, turned on their rulers. Plots, public executions and petty theft surged, as people within the city took the side of the French and the English, and acted as spies, collaborators and, at times, assassins.

'The city's charnel houses and cemeteries overflowed with corpses.'

Amid this, a comet was reported hovering over the city for three days, and the Black Death struck Paris. Arriving from the east and landing first in Marseille, the bubonic plague obliterated the population. Its victims presented symptoms such as black boils, swellings and sores in the groin and armpits. Doctors could neither understand nor cure it, of course, but so-called 'plague doctors' were only too willing to try.

Dressed in protective clothing that included bird-like masks with long noses, the doctors tried lancing the boils, blood-letting and feeding the victims foul-tasting concoctions cooked up by alchemists. Many of these quacks were soon suffering from plague symptoms themselves, as were the city's Augustin nuns, who did their best to comfort the dying.

DESCRIPTION OF THE PLAGUE

Jean de Venette was a friar from the Carmelite monastery in the Place Maubert when the bubonic plague swept Paris. This is how he described the events:

'All this year and the next, the mortality of men and women, of the young even more than of the old, in Paris and in the kingdom of France, and also, it is said, in other parts of the world, was so great that it was almost impossible to bury the dead. People lay ill little more than two or three days and died suddenly, as it were in full health. He who was well one day was dead the next and being carried to his grave. Swellings appeared suddenly in the armpit or in the groin – in many cases both – and they were infallible signs of death. This sickness or pestilence was called an epidemic by the doctors. Nothing like the great numbers who died in the years 1348 and 1349 has been heard of or seen of in times past.' (Jean de Venette, *The Chronicle*, translated by Jean Birdsall)

Paris could not cope with the sheer numbers of the dead, which at the peak reached more than 700 a day. The city's charnel houses and cemeteries overflowed with corpses; soon bodies were simply left to rot in the street. Those who could leave the city did so. Those who were stricken with the disease often locked themselves away and prayed, until they too were taken. Others, declaring the end of the world had come, fell into public drunkenness, fornication, and other forms of vice.

Many Parisians, believing the disease to be a punishment from God, took to redeeming themselves by burning lepers and Jews, well-known apostles of hell. Cats, also thought to be evil, were thrown onto the pyres, thus ensuring that the rats that were carrying the plague thrived. Then, finally, the disease finished its devastation in the winter of 1349.

Finding Paris

The Hundred Years' War was quick to start up again after the end of the Black Death. As the war continued on its confused and convoluted path, Paris began to form something akin to a recognized civic identity, one that was bound up in the revolt and political insurrection that so often defined the city. A new round of unrest followed the attempts of the new French king John II to control the city's criminal forces, while also imposing new taxes to pay for his war against the English.

Paris at that time was full of undesirables – army deserters,

ABOVE: The Danse Macabré, or the 'Dance of Death', is an artistic genre that first appeared in murals painted around Parisian plague pits. The Danse Macabré is an allegorical reference to the universality of death, which unites all.

prostitutes, thieves, murderers and quacks – who had virtual control of the streets. The bourgeoisie, meanwhile, suffered because the monarch failed to provide certain civic fundamentals, such as law and order and a tax system free from sudden and arbitrary hikes.

The rise to fame of one of Paris' most famous medieval rabble-rousers, Étienne Marcel, began in 1355 when he was elected Alderman of the City. Marcel won popular acclaim by proposing the people of Paris do away with interfering rulers and corrupt tax officials and take control of their own destiny. He created militias made up of 3000 of the city's citizens and rebuilt the city's fortifications. He even wrote a new constitution and seized the Louvre Palace, where, in a portent of the revolutionary events of 1789 and 1871, he declared that a Commune of Paris should govern itself. To underline his independence, Marcel then had two of

Here, Étienne Marcel shows the *dauphin* the murdered bodies of the city marshals in his curbing of royal authority. In the end, Marcel's extremism would be his undoing.

Charles VI et les Parisiens en armes.

the city marshals butchered in front of the *dauphin* ('heir apparent'), soon to be Charles V of France. He dressed the *dauphin* in a red and blue hood – the colours adopted for Marcel's emblem – and paraded him over the corpses of the marshals.

The killings and the *dauphin's* humiliation was a costly blunder that fatally undermined Marcel's credibility. The *dauphin* left Paris to drum up support and Marcel sent some of his Paris militia to aid a peasant uprising north of the city. When this revolt was quelled, Marcel's popularity diminished, and the leader resorted to seeking help from the English before being finally assassinated. Now, the *dauphin* crept back into Paris apologetically; the city was quick to forgive him. In turn, the *dauphin* promised there would be fewer executions and no immediate rise in taxes. The people responded by helping to raise the ransom for King John II, at the time incarcerated in a London jail.

But despite these appearances of harmony, Marcel's uprising had severely damaged relations between the *dauphin* and his capital-to-be. On becoming Charles V after John II's death in 1364, the king built a new palace at Saint-Pol heavily protected by the new Bastille fortress. Charles had no intention of being dictated to by his subjects; neither were the people of Paris finished with popular uprisings against those in the seat of power.

'Paris would teeter between royal control and anarchic chaos for over a century.'

Paris would teeter awkwardly between royal control and anarchic chaos for over a century. After Charles V's death in 1380, a meeting of the Estates General demanded the abolition of royal taxes: street riots and a round of rebel executions followed. Charles' successor, Charles VI, was so insane that he imagined his bones were made of glass and ordered his clothes be fitted with iron rods so he could stand upright. The instability of Charles' rule led to war between his two brothers, the Duke of Bourgogne, leader of the Burgundians, and the Duke of Orleans, leader of the Armagnacs.

The Burgundians, the Armagnacs, the English, and the soldiers of Charles VI made up the various factions that occupied Paris during the Hundred Years' War, each bringing bloodshed and misery upon the city until the end of the war in 1453. During this time, the *Journal d'un Bourgeois de Paris*, written by two priests between 1409 and 1449, recounts the grim daily existence familiar to many Parisians. The journal recorded eight years of epidemics, four years of flooding, several years of harsh winter frosts, plagues of crop-killing beetles, impossibly high tax rises, and – worst of all – the unforgivable English culinary habit of boiling meat.

Paris and France would eventually emerge as a unified nation under Charles VII, who was crowned in 1429 and ousted the English from their last stronghold in Calais in 1453. Paris had somehow kept itself from the brink of destruction and emerged with a Parisian character that is still celebrated today. From the fifteenth century, texts such as the *Journal d'un Bourgeois de Paris* referred to 'Parisian' not only as a member of the capital city, but as a unique individual with a particular way of behaving and thinking.

In sixteenth-century Paris, however, the ideals of the individual once again gave way to the mentality of the mob. The city, like so many others across Europe at the time, became a hotbed of religious extremism, as Catholic fundamentalists raged violently against French Protestants, known as the Huguenots. The subsequent 37-year conflict, which killed millions through war, famine and disease, became known to history as the French Wars of Religion.

OPPOSITE: Here, Charles VI attempts to quell an uprising during one of his periods of sanity. In his more unsettled moments, Charles 'the Mad' would attack servants, run until exhausted, and forget his own name.

WARS OF RELIGION

Sixteenth-century Paris was considered a city on heat. It held a reputation as the European centre of sin and hedonism, a carnal capital open to every depravity. At the top was François I, a king famous for moral squalor and debauchery. Below were François' subjects, who shared their sovereign's appetites.

Thousands of prostitutes from around the continent flocked to Paris. Most of these women worked in and around Notre Dame Cathedral, earning good incomes from distracted churchgoers. Many blamed the Italians for the decadence: sixteenth-century Paris was a city that borrowed heavily from the artistic and cultural ideals of its Renaissance neighbours. François I was greatly influenced by the Italian style: he spared no expense decking out his court with an opulence worthy of Rome; he wore the latest fashions cut from the finest cloth; he bought paintings by the popular Leonardo da Vinci; and he invited the outrageous Italian sculptor Benvenuto Cellini to become a familiar of his entourage.

For many Parisians, Cellini was a figure of hatred and derision. He was flamboyant, dangerous and appeared to encourage François in the debauchery considered to be ruining France. Only a century earlier, Cellini would have been charged with heresy and his corpse hung high with dozens of others on the Gibbet of Montfaucon. Instead, Cellini's exploits served as entertainment for François'

OPPOSITE: As a child François I was infatuated with chivalrous romances and the pomp and ceremony of royal life. As king he would fill his court with scholars, artists, rough noblemen and beautiful women, and indulge every appetite. His nickname was 'Francis of the Big Nose'.

ABOVE: This sixteenth century map, showing the medieval boundaries of Paris, was one of hundreds of bird-eye views of cities produced by cartographers Georg Braun and Franz Hogenberg in their *Civitates orbis terrarum*.

courtiers, whose orgies were notorious. Foreign dignitaries were shocked to witness civilized dinners held by the city's aristocracy descend into drunken bacchanalia.

For privileged Parisian aristocrats, Cellini was considered the model for the raffish gentleman of the sixteenth century. Many Catholics were disgusted by him, not only because they held him partly responsible for the unchristian lust and licentiousness sweeping Paris, but also because he was a Protestant sympathizer.

Religion lay at the heart of the real tension bubbling beneath the surface. Paris, like France around it, was a conservative Catholic heartland facing a perilous new threat: Protestantism. For Catholics, Protestantism was the new heresy that wouldn't die. It started in 1520 when Martin Luther had been excommunicated for nailing 95 theses to a church door in Wittenberg attacking the corruptions of the Catholic Church.

Martin Luther and his Protestantism was of great interest to nobles such as François I, who felt suffocated by Catholic conservatism. For François, Protestantism represented a religion that was fresh and free-thinking, just as Italy had provided the model for living without boundaries. François lived a life of grandiose self-indulgence, travelling everywhere with a splendid retinue of wives, mistresses, tapestries, gold plates, and a herd of horses to transport them all. A new addition to his court was Catherine de Médicis, an exotic Italian François had invited to Paris to marry his son Henri, which earned her the nickname 'the king's whore'.

Catherine was an apostle of the new morality imported from Italy: she dressed in the high heels normally favoured by prostitutes, used sex as a way of securing deals and loyalties, and was allegedly involved in the dark arts. Catherine surrounded herself with an entourage that included astrologers, alchemists, and nine dwarves who travelled in their own miniature coaches. Also attending Catherine were around 80 ladies-in-waiting known as her 'flying squadron', who traded sex for political gain. On one occasion, Catherine invited a host of dignitaries to a banquet where the flying squadron served the meal topless before granting after-dinner favours. Catherine also held large spectacles outside the city, including a mock battle between her servants dressed as Trojans and Greeks overlooked by a tower of scantily clad nymphs. Catherine had a habit of poisoning those who displeased her; she dispatched one of her own astrologers this way, remarking that he 'should have seen it coming'.

Catherine, however, was of no interest to her husband Henri, who became King Henri II after François' death in 1547. Henri showered gifts upon his

CELLINI THE CAD

Cellini was a freewheeling cad and philanderer who moved in aristocratic circles in both Italy and France. Although his sculptures were considered masterpieces, Cellini spent much of his time involved in sword fighting, fornication and even murder. According to his own autobiography, he beat women, killed men in duels, and once attacked the Parisian *prévôt* for not vacating an apartment promised to him by François I.

Cellini often took his young models as mistresses and was charged with the act of sodomy four times: once with a woman and three times with men, including his apprentice. However, any moves to take legal action against Cellini were often met with violence, as he explains:

'When certain decisions of the court were sent me by those lawyers, and I perceived that my cause had been unjustly lost, I had recourse for my defence to a great dagger which I carried; for I have always taken pleasure in keeping fine weapons. The first man I attacked was the plaintiff who had sued me; and one evening I wounded him in the legs and arms so severely, taking care, however, not to kill him, that I deprived him of the use of both his legs. Then I sought out the other fellow who had brought the suit, and used him also in such wise that he dropped it.' (Benvenuto Cellini, *Autobiography*, translated by J.A. Symonds)

ABOVE: Despite his reputation for violence and sexual deviancy, Cellini was a legitimate artist who helped pioneer the Mannerist style.

mistress and sat on her knee and fondled her breasts in front of Catherine. Catherine assumed part of the problem was her inability to produce an heir. She had tried everything to correct this, including drinking mule's urine and smearing her genitals with cow's dung; these measures had little effect. However, after 10 years of trying, Catherine fell pregnant and then went on to give birth to 10 of Henri's children. Three of these children would become kings of France. However, it was Catherine, and not her husband, who would go on to become the most powerful figure in French politics of the time.

Catherine's moment began when Henri was killed during a jousting accident in 1559. An opponent's lance had splintered during the tournament and put out Henri's eye, leading to fatal septicaemia. Despite the fact that Henri was wearing the colours of his mistress, Catherine was said to genuinely grieve for her husband's demise; she ordered his palace to be razed in his honour.

Henri's widow would oversee one of the most violent and turbulent periods in Parisian and French history: The Wars of Religion, fought between the Protestant Huguenots and the Catholics, a conflict that would split the population in two and ravage the country for more than three decades.

The Wars Begin

François I was one French king who had changed his religion to suit his purposes; he would not be the last. The Protestant king converted to Catholicism under pressure from his mother and the Church, and following a stint in a Spanish jail. Under François' son, Henri II, the persecution of Protestants began in

ABOVE: Known as 'the king's whore', Catherine de Médicis would often trade the sexual favours of her ladies in waiting for political gain. She became one of the most powerful figures of sixteenth century Europe.

OPPOSITE: Here, Henri is attended to after having his eye punctured by the splinter from a lance. The infected wound would later cost him his life.

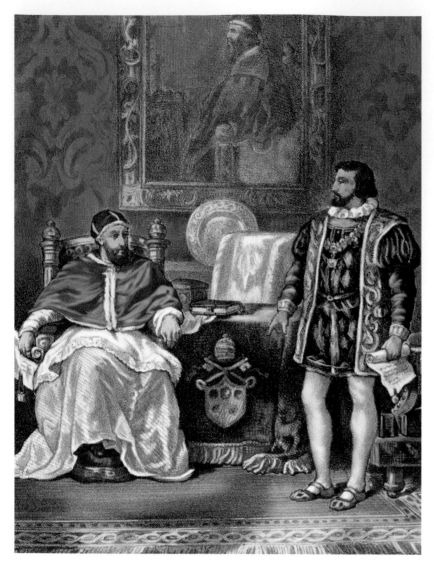

ABOVE: Here, François I suggests to Pope Clement VII that he call a meeting between Catholic and Protestant rulers to work out their differences. The suggestion was not well received.

earnest. Catholicism had the support of Spain, Italy and the powerful Guise family: its roots went deep in France. However, Protestantism had gained fresh support among many members of the French nobility with the advent of Calvinism, a more austere form of Protestantism.

The Sorbonne saw itself as the great upholder of Catholicism in Paris and used intimidation and violence in its persecution of Protestants. Students at the Sorbonne raided Protestant gatherings and slaughtered all participants, including women. This vigilante behaviour was encouraged by the *prévôt*, who considered the killings a lessening of his own workload. Those found guilty of heresy would face, at best, prison or deportation; at worst, public torture and death by immolation.

An early outbreak of Protestant militancy against the Catholic persecutions came on 18 October 1534, the 'Day of the Placards'. On this day the city awoke to find Protestant placards posted around the city denouncing the Catholic doctrine of the mass. One of the placards had even been nailed to the door of the king's bedchamber. It has been claimed that the Day of the Placards turned Protestantism into a 'religion for rebels', and it certainly saw a hardening of the already uncompromising Catholic line on heresy. Around 500 Protestant 'heretics' were put to death in the first three years of Henri II's reign alone.

Another atrocity against Protestants occurred outside Paris in 1562 in the town of Wassy. Like many French towns, the population of Wassy was split into Catholics and Protestants. It was also ruled over by a Catholic zealot, the Duc de Guise. While out with his men one day, the Duc chanced upon a group of Protestants holding a secret service in a barn near the town. A scuffle broke out and the Duc suffered a wound to his eye. Outraged, he ordered his men to surround the town and set fire to the barn, killing 63 Protestants and injuring 100 more. The massacre sparked confrontations between the religious factions around the country, and is considered the starting point of the Wars of Religion.

THE CATHOLIC TERROR

The *prévôt* of Paris, John Morin, began the Catholic retaliation for the Protestant Day of the Placards a few weeks after they appeared. Morin's method was to torture one Protestant until he confessed and then identified another involved in the crime. He then marched the informant to the home of the accused and had him arrested in full view of the street. The trials for the placard Protestants began on 10 November and the executions by immolation began three days later. The killings lasted for several weeks and were spread around the city so all could bear witness to them. To create a feeling of camaraderie among the Catholics, candle-lit processions were staged through the streets of Paris. Holy relics from the city's churches were featured in these parades, including the head of Saint Louis, a piece of the true cross, the alleged crown of thorns, a nail from Christ's cross, the towel that Christ wore at the Last Supper, some of Christ's baby clothes, and the spearhead that had pierced his side on the cross.

In selected sites along the processional route Protestant executions took place, as this eyewitness account records:

'The men set apart to death were first to undergo prolonged and excruciating torture and for this end a most ingenious device had been devised. First rose an upright beam planted in the ground, to that another beam

was attached crosswise and worked with a pulley and string. The martyr was fastened to one end of the movable beam by his hands which were tied behind his back and then he was raised into the air. He was then let down into the slow fire underneath. After a minute's broiling he was raised again and a second time dropped into the fire, and was thus raised and lowered until the ropes that fastened him to the pole were consumed and he fell into the burning coal where he lay till he gave up the ghost.' (Johann Sleidan, *History of the Reformation*, translated by G. Bohun)

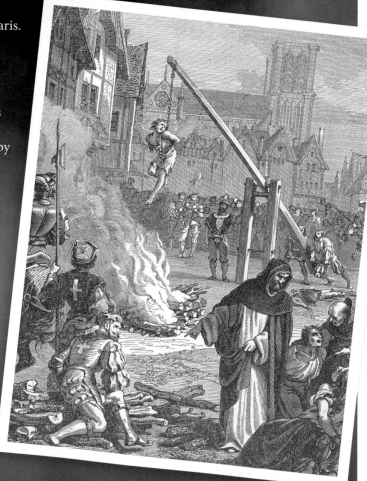

RIGHT: Public immolation was a common punishment for Parisian Protestants found guilty of heresy.

The Massacre of Wassy was only one of several massacres to take place against French Protestants and was by no means the largest. However, it sent a stream of Protestant refugees into the city of Paris, some to seek shelter and safety, others to mount a direct challenge to the Guise family and the Pope himself.

'The violence was fuelled by alcohol and focused initially on members of the public.'

Sectarian violence became just another aspect of everyday Parisian life until Catherine de Médicis issued an edict that allowed for Protestant worship in the privacy of their own homes. Catherine had taken over as regent of France in place of her son Charles IX, who was only 10 years old when he succeeded his dead brother François II in 1560. Catherine's aim was to walk the middle line between the two religious factions and to work out an amicable solution acceptable to both sides. Failing this, she would attempt to unite the factions under the rule of the crown through the time-honoured diplomatic manoeuvre of a royal marriage.

The marriage that Catherine decided to broker was between Marguerite de Valois, a Catholic royal, and Henri de Navarre, a Protestant aristocrat who would later become Henri IV. Catherine sent invitations to all of the great aristocratic families of France and organized for lavish banquets, parties and balls to be held throughout Paris, celebrations that contrasted sharply with the abject poverty

BELOW: After discovering Protestants worshipping in a barn, the Duc de Guise ordered the group killed and the building razed. The resulting Massacre of Wassy sparked the Wars of Religion.

Die von der reformierten religion zu Vaßij. Seint in irer predigh am ersten tag Martij.

Durch des hertzogen von Guise gebott. Erschoßen geschlagen vnd gestochen zu todt.

Mann, Weib vnd kinde ohn vnterscheyt. Mit wutender grim vnd grausamkeyt.

Welches dem Cardinal von Lotharing. Nach seines hertzen wunsch erging.

Am I. Mart. M. D. LXII.

suffered by many Parisians. Despite this, the capital on Saint Bartholomew's Eve, 1572, became packed with both Protestants and Catholics alike, to witness the wedding in a public square outside Notre Dame cathedral. What followed was one of the most savage and sustained massacres ever to strike a capital city in Europe.

The Saint Bartholomew Massacre

It is unclear who gave the order for the massacre of Paris' Protestants by the city's Catholics led by the Duc of Guise. According to legend, it was Charles IX who commanded 'Kill them all, so no-one will be left to reproach me for it.' There is also strong evidence that Charles' mother, Catherine de Médicis , played a part, in particular by ordering the assassination of Admiral Gaspard de Coligny, a Protestant sympathizer who was well liked by his men. Catherine felt that if Coligny turned against the crown he could pose a real threat to the continuation of the Valois line.

The slaying of Coligny and several other high-profile Parisian Protestants signalled the start of a merciless slaughter across the city, as religious hatred, xenophobia, and old rivalries were settled in blood over the day and night that followed. The violence was fuelled by alcohol and focused initially on members of the public who had come out to enjoy the wedding celebrations: unarmed men, women, children, and the elderly. The city was soon littered with corpses, which lay where they fell or were dragged through the streets to be thrown into the Seine. Eyewitnesses describe the river being choked with corpses and the water running red with blood. Large pits were dug in green spaces so the cadavers could be buried quickly.

Houses were sacked and burned; rich Protestants were offered the chance to pay for their lives; other Protestants were forced to recite the mass before meeting their end. Sometimes the killing was designed to mimic the sentence for heresy – being burned alive. Many of the murders were choreographed, with 5000 militiamen commanded by 150 captains in turn led by the Duc of Guise. Each captain was responsible for a particular *dizaine* – the immediate area around a particular street – and the mobilization of its inhabitants. Many historians believe the massacre was premeditated and planned years in advance; the spontaneous violence of the mob simply added to the slaughter. The crowd celebrated when a decrepit hawthorn bush in the Cemetery of the Innocents suddenly burst into life: this miracle, they said, was a sign that God was pleased with their actions.

ABOVE: Here, Henri de Navarre, the future Henri IV, courts his betrothed Marguerite de Valois. Their wedding at Notre Dame would become the setting for the bloodsoaked Saint Bartholomew massacre of the city's Protestants.

The slaying of Admiral Gaspard de Coligny, whose corpse is shown hanging from a window, began the Saint Bartholomew massacre. Catherine de Médicis emerges from the Louvre to inspect a pile of Protestant bodies.

THE MURDER OF COLIGNY

French statesman Jacques Auguste de Thou, who witnessed the massacre as a young man, recounts Coligny's death in his *History of his Own Time*, a publication banned by the Catholic Church:

ABOVE: Before his death, Coligny reputedly shouted: "Would that I might at least die at the hands of a soldier and not of a valet."

'Meanwhile the conspirators, having burst through the door of the chamber, entered, and when Besme, sword in hand, had demanded of Coligny, who stood near the door, "Are you Coligny ?" Coligny replied, "Yes, I am he," with fearless countenance. "But you, young man, respect these white hairs. What is it you would do? You cannot shorten by many days this life of mine." As he spoke, Besme gave him a sword thrust through the body, and having withdrawn his sword, another thrust in the mouth, by which his face was disfigured. So Coligny fell, killed with many thrusts…Then the Duc of Guise inquired of Besme from the courtyard if the thing were done, and when Besme answered him that it was, the Duc replied that the Chevalier d'Angoulême was unable to believe it unless he saw it; and at the same time that he made the inquiry they threw the body through the window into the courtyard, disfigured as it was with blood. When the Chevalier d'Angoulême, who could scarcely believe his eyes, had wiped away with a cloth the blood which overran the face and finally had recognized him, some say that he spurned the body with his foot. However this may be, when he left the house with his followers he said: "Cheer up, my friends! Let us do thoroughly that which we have begun. The king commands it." He frequently repeated these words, and as soon as they had caused the bell of the palace clock to ring, on every side arose the cry, "To arms!" and the people ran to the house of Coligny. After his body had been treated to all sorts of insults, they threw it into a neighbouring stable, and finally cut off his head, which they sent to Rome. They also mutilated him, and dragged his body through the streets to the bank of the Seine, a thing which he had formerly almost prophesied. As some children were in the act of throwing the body into the river, it was dragged out and placed upon the gibbet of Montfaucon, where it hung by the feet in chains of iron; and then they built a fire beneath, by which he was burned without being consumed; so that he was, so to speak, tortured with all the elements, since he was killed upon the earth, thrown into the water, placed upon the fire, and finally put to hang in the air.' (Jacques Auguste de Thou, *History of his Own Time*, translated by Samuel Buckley)

The violence soon spread to other cities, where similar Protestant massacres were recorded. None, however could match the five-day orgy of death in Paris, where up to 30,000 were murdered in the name of God.

If the Catholic mob of Paris believed the Saint Bartholomew's Day Massacre would reform the royal court and end the decadence of the city, they were wrong. Henri III was the last ruler of the Valois dynasty and would scandalize the throne in ways previously unknown.

Another son of Catherine de Médicis, Henri had come to the throne under murky circumstances after the death of his brother, Charles IX. Charles had officially died of tuberculosis, but many suspected he had been poisoned by Catherine herself, who considered him a liability. Charles had always had a delicate constitution and apparently felt guilty over the Saint Bartholomew's Day Massacre, often ranting to his mother: 'What bloodshed! What murders! What evil counsel I have followed… Who but you is the cause of all of this? God's blood, you are the cause of it all!' Catherine would respond by calling Charles a lunatic, but she would not bear the sounds of his lamentations for long.

Charles' brother Henri III was a foppish and flamboyant ruler who outraged his subjects by flaunting his bisexuality and dressing in drag. Nicknamed the 'King of Sodom', Henri spent every waking moment among a tight retinue of young effeminates called *mignons*, or 'little cuties'. To the public, the *mignons*

'They also shamefully mutilated him and dragged his body through the streets.'

BELOW: Henri III and his mother Catherine de Médicis attend a ball at the royal palace. By dressing in drag and surrounding himself with effeminates, Henri made himself a figure of ridicule among his people.

represented everything that was wrong with France and its rulers. Paris had an international reputation for murder and treason, with 'Parisian' a byword for depravity, fanaticism and murder. Intended as a term of abuse, this use of 'Parisian' contained a core of truth. The violent immorality of the elite was shared by the people.

BELOW: Paul Stuart de Caussade de Saint-Mégrin, here modelling the popular fashion of Henri III's court, was one of the king's favourite *mignons*.

The Mignons

Henri III's *mignons* were much derided by ordinary Parisians, who blamed them for the king's effeminacy and his penchant for dressing as a woman at court. The journal of Pierre de L'Estoile provides a popular account:

'The mignons began to be much talked about by the common people, who hated them not only because of their foolish and haughty ways and of their effeminate and immodest make-up and clothes, but above all for the huge gifts heaped upon them by the king. The people blamed them for their impoverishment… These pretty mignons had their hair pomaded, curled and recurled and tied over small bonnets in the manner of prostitutes. Their shirt collars were so stiff and wide that their heads looked like that of St John on the platter… Their favourite pastimes were gambling, blaspheming, leaping, dancing, pirouetting, quarrelling and wenching.' (Pierre de L'Estoile, *Memoires-Journal*, translated by Nancy Roelker)

The streets of Paris were ruled by an army of beggars, prostitutes, hustlers, thieves, drunks and soldiers on the loose. Many of these soldiers had not been paid in months and carried out robberies at bayonet point, drinking their booty and raping women in the street. Dozens of bridges and alleyways were known no-go areas; most law-abiding Parisians did not venture outside after dark.

Robbery was rife in Paris, with thieves organized into particular roles. These included beggars who only worked part-time during the winter; thieves who pretended to have been robbed as their accomplices held up at knife-point passers-by wishing to help; and those who extorted money from well-meaning Christians by presenting papers that proved their house had burned down.

Many people blamed Henri III for the depraved behaviour on the streets; others pointed at his mother, Catherine de Médicis. Xenophobia added to the religious intolerance at this time, and foreigners were to be feared and hated. When Catherine died in 1589, the Parisian public wanted her body thrown into the Seine, the gravest of insults. Isolated in a growing power struggle between the court and the Guise family's powerful Catholic League, Henri was assassinated.

Paris celebrated Henri's death, and paraded through the streets shouting 'the tyrant is dead'. During the traditional mourning period, the city took on a festival atmosphere and kept the streets lamps burning so they could celebrate at night. Many spat on the corpse of the king interred at the Church of Les Cordeliers. The governorship of Paris then fell into the hands of the Catholic League and its Council of Sixteen, which immediately promised to rid the city of its Protestants once and for all. Henri's successor, Henri IV, a Huguenot, would have to win his new capital city by force.

Paris Besieged

Henri IV, formerly known as Henri of Navarre, had celebrated his wedding day in Paris some 18 years earlier, the fateful event that would herald the Saint Bartholomew's Day Massacre. Now, in March 1590, as king of France, he stood outside the city gates at the head of an army intending to storm the city. Henri had burned the nearby windmills and fields and aimed to starve the city out. He split his men into divisions so they could surround the city; the wait, Henri told them, would be a matter of weeks rather than months.

Paris, however, had seen Henri coming and had stocked the city larders well. Those inside felt confident they could outlast the king who, through his scorched earth policy, had deprived himself of the food source that had lain at his feet. Henri had brought with him an army of around 12,000 soldiers to besiege a city of 200,000, which included a garrison of around 50,000 men. To bombard the city, Henri had brought a dozen cannons that he set up on the Montmartre hill and commenced firing. Cannon in the sixteenth century were clumsy, inaccurate and had poor range; mirth rather than fear over Henri's efforts was the overriding emotion from the besieged Parisians.

Henri was inexperienced as a king, but had a mule-like stubbornness: he was willing to play the long game. Three months of siege left Paris starving and desperate. People had begun eating their mules, horses and goats; then they turned to cats, dogs and other small animals, roasting them on spits in the city's squares. An eyewitness account reported a group descending on a dead dog in the gutter and devouring its entrails and brains raw.

Soon there were dozens dying each day and bodies piled up in the streets. Many had suffered from dropsy, a disease that distends the stomach. People were reported to be eating candle wax, grass, wooden furniture and even boiling fur coats for broth. Some had begun exhuming the dead from the cemetery and grinding their bones to make flour; others had resorted to cannibalism, with the

ABOVE: Despite Catherine de Médicis' best efforts to curb Henri III's excesses and make him a model king, both royals were hated by the public at the time of their deaths.

THE ASSASSINATION OF HENRI III

'It was about 8 a.m. when the king, sitting naked on his close stool except for a dressing gown over his shoulders, was informed that a monk from Paris wished to speak to him. Hearing that his guards were barring the monk's way, he angrily ordered the monk to be admitted, saying that otherwise he would be accused in Paris of chasing monks away. The Jacobin, with a knife hidden up his sleeve, entered and introduced himself to the king, who having just risen, had not yet fastened his breeches. After making a deep bow, the monk handed to the king a letter from the count of Brienne… The king, believing he was in no danger, ordered his attendants to withdraw.

He opened the letter and began reading it, whereupon the monk, seizing the king thus engrossed pulled out his knife and plunged it deeply into the king's abdomen just above the navel. With a great effort the king pulled it out and struck the monk's left eyebrow with its point. At the same time he shouted: "Ah! The wicked monk has killed me! Kill him!" The king's guards and others hearing his shouts, rushed into the room and felled the Jacobin at the king's feet… That night, His Majesty, seeing his life was ebbing away, asked for a mass to be said in his chamber and took communion.' (Pierre de l'Estoile, *Memoires-Journal*, translated by Nancy Roelker)

limbs of children chopped up and disguised as game. Meanwhile, it was reported that the church had food to spare and was selling to rich Parisians at extortionate prices. Tens of thousands died during the siege; some estimates place the death toll at more than 50,000. Paris seemed doomed to fall to the king. Those left alive prepared themselves for a retaliatory slaughter worthy of Saint Bartholomew. Then in late September, a miracle came.

'There was little he could do but call off the siege. Paris was saved.'

Help was delivered along the Parisian artery that had so long been the lifeblood of the city – the Seine. Spanish army boats heavy with grain and other provisions reached the Île de la Cité under the nose of Henri's army. For Henri, it was a disaster – there was little he could do but call off the siege. Paris was saved.

In 1591, he tried a Trojan horse tactic by sending a contingent of men to the city gates disguised as peasants carrying flour. The soldiers were let in and quickly slaughtered, the flour kept as a reward. It eventually dawned on Henri that he would have to change tactics if he wanted to sit upon his Parisian throne.

This was the moment the king uttered his infamous words 'Paris is worth a mass'. Like François I before him, Henri agreed to abjure Protestantism and become a Catholic. So it was that in 1593 Henri was converted at a ceremony at Saint Denis, before tens of thousands of Parisians who had sneaked out of the city for the occasion. Henri faced hard negotiations with the Catholic League over the terms of the surrender of Paris. In the end only 140 of the League's members would suffer any long-term punishment; most were banished from the city. Finally, in March 1594, Henri marched into his capital as King of France. After a prayer in Notre Dame Cathedral, he led a procession of his citizens to his residence at the Louvre Palace. Paris, at last, had a king; and peace.

OPPOSITE: Henri IV is welcomed into the capital after admitting 'Paris is worth a mass' and converting to Catholicism. His first stop as he entered the city was at Notre Dame for prayer.

The New Paris

Henri's capital in 1594 was far removed from the grand, architecturally designed marvel that he would leave behind. Decades of warfare and misery had left the city devastated, its infrastructure broken. Many of the city's buildings had been destroyed and most of its churches were in ruins. The streets, paved by Philippe Auguste in the thirteenth century, were covered in a thick layer of mud, rotting rubbish and human excrement. Horses often broke their legs in the large, sludge-filled potholes; in the rain it was impossible to walk without getting covered in black street slime.

The city's sanitation had also fallen into decline, there was no workable sewer system and the city's fountains had run dry. The river once again became the main source of the city's fresh water supply, and a convenient dumping point for effluent not simply thrown into the street. Fresh water was therefore usually

BELOW: The Catholic League, here in procession, was formed by the Duc de Guise to usurp the authority of Henri II and rid Paris of its Protestants.

contaminated and disease in the city was endemic; tens of thousands fell prey to a plague in 1580 alone.

Services in Paris were non-existent and commerce had ground to halt: shop fronts were boarded up and fresh supplies were scarce. Parisians were told not to leave their homes completely uninhabited, as bands of aggressive beggars combed the streets looking for opportunities to loot. Medieval tortures, such as the rack and wheel, were used on criminals found guilty of robbery and bodily harm; those of the higher classes were granted the privilege of decapitation.

Physically, Paris itself was more or less the same city it had been in medieval times: a grey, walled city encircled by fortifications and with the Île de la Cité at its heart. Large wooden bridges across the river were crammed with houses, squalid death traps prone to fire or flood, or sudden collapse into the river. Henri had pledged to remove these bridges and replace them with wide, stone

ABOVE: Catholic fanatic François Ravaillac attacks Henri IV's carriage during his assassination of the king. Henri's new, armoured Italian carriage was not employed on that day.

versions without housing. The most famous of these bridges was the Pont Neuf, which immediately took on the status of a busy town square: citizens would venture there to stroll, buy and sell goods, or hire a prostitute.

The Pont Neuf was only one of many projects in Henri's grand plan to rebuild Paris as the jewel of Europe. Taking his lead from the Italian classical style, Henri ordered his city to be remade with brick, stone and marble. Like Philippe Auguste before him, Henri loved Paris and laboured to transform it. He extended the Louvre, built public fountains, constructed the Place Dauphine, and created a small park, known today as the Square du Vert-Galant, by the Seine's Right Bank.

Henri built the square as a sort of outside boudoir, an open space where the king could cavort with mistresses and ladies of the night. Today the square retains a reputation for certain open-air liaisons. Henri himself was notorious for his libidinous appetites: despite reportedly having the odour of a goat, he was adored by women, had many affairs and mistresses, and was linked to a variety of sexual scandals. Most Parisians turned a blind eye to the king's excesses; the stalwarts of the Catholic League did not. The League had shrunk from a legitimate order to an underground terror cell, fomenting revolt and enlisting disaffected Catholics as royal assassins.

For many, 'Good King Henri', as he was known, was simply the saviour of France. The ensuing 16 years of his rule was considered something of a golden era after the turbulence of the Religious Wars. The king's Edict of Nantes laid out the terms of peaceful cohabitation between French Catholics and Protestants; he had created great building works that restored the Parisians' pride in their capital; and more broadly, he had brought peace to the country. Then, in 1610, Henri's reign was brought suddenly to a brutal, blood soaked end.

In the middle of the seventeenth century, another uprising would plunge France and its capital city into chaos and disorder once more. This conflict, a civil war known as 'The Fronde', would cement the power of the king as an absolute monarch, and later pave the way for the greatest Parisian insurrection of all, the French Revolution of 1789.

THE MURDER OF HENRI IV

Henri had survived at least two dozen assassination attempts since his coronation, but still treated his personal safety with a certain nonchalance. His closest courtiers did what they could to protect him. A new carriage surrounded with glass windows – a kind of Renaissance-style Popemobile – had just been shipped in from Italy. Unfortunately, Henri had chosen an older, flimsier carriage with open windows to navigate the narrow city streets of Paris on his journey on 14 May 1610.

Also out that day was François Ravaillac, a failed priest and schoolteacher conscripted by the Catholic League to kill the king. Ravaillac was a fanatical Catholic given to hallucinations of the battlefields of God and great heretic massacres. He had tried for several days to be granted an audience with Henri before wandering the city streets. On 14 May, he procured a large kitchen knife.

Henri's carriage had been brought to a stop in the rue de la Ferronnerie behind a broken cart when Ravaillac approached. He jumped into the royal carriage and delivered three thrusts, one of which stabbed Henri through the heart. Ravaillac made no move to run and was grabbed by Henri's assistants, but the king was gone.

For his regicide, Ravaillac would be made to suffer the most violent of tortures. On 27 May, on a scaffold in front of a jeering crowd, Ravaillac was scalded, his flesh shredded with red-hot pincers, and boiling oil poured into the wounds. He was then tied to four horses, which took 30 minutes to tear his body apart. Then the crowd descended on what was left, hacking, battering and slashing at the dismembered limbs and dragging them through the streets. Pieces of flesh were thrown onto bonfires and one woman was even reported to have eaten the charred flesh.

BELOW: During Ravaillac's execution, one of the horses faltered and needed to be replaced with a more vigorous beast.

REVOLUTIONS AND THE ANCIEN RÉGIME

Louis XIV hated Paris. One of his early memories of the city was of feigning sleep when an angry mob burst into his palace. Louis retreated from the people into a gilded cage in Versailles, becoming the ruling despot of the *ancien régime*. This in turn would lead to the most notorious revolution in world history.

IT IS AN irony that the moment that so traumatized Louis, a sovereign famous for living extravagantly at the expense of his people, arose over a rise in taxation. A mob took up arms and stormed the royal residence of the Palais-Royal, demanding to see their king-to-be. One entered the royal bedchamber. Here, on his mother's advice, nine-year-old Louis pretended to be asleep. Pacified, the mob left the palace. It was a seminal moment that shaped all of Louis' future policies. Crowned in 1654, Louis would style himself as the 'Sun King', whose right to rule was given by God. His reign lasted for 72 years, the longest of any European monarch, and he ruled unfettered by the people. Louis devoted himself to power and earthly pleasure.

The *ancien régime*, however, eventually collapsed under the weight of its own oppression. In centralizing the power of France under one man, Louis sidelined all democratic institutions, alienated his powerful nobility, and ignored the plight of the common man. The final consequence was the French Revolution of 1789 and the death of the French monarchy.

OPPOSITE: Versailles was a whole royal town built away from the troubles of Paris. At the geographical centre of Louis XIV's palace was his bedroom, the heart of a courtly hive of ceremony and control.

As the successor to Cardinal Richelieu, Cardinal Mazarin's main priority was to eliminate domestic opposition to the king while increasing his supremacy among the powers of Europe.

The Fronde

The tax rises that sparked the storming of the Palais-Royal reflected the extravagance of the Bourbons, the royal family of which Louis was born. The Bourbons had spent recklessly on lavish building works in Paris; continuing wars with Spain and Austria had also helped break the bank

To pay the bill, Cardinal Mazarin, the king's chief minister, introduced a series of taxes between 1644 and 1648. Mazarin justified the taxes by saying that the French aristocracy generally could afford it. The Parlement of Paris, a law court made up of aristocrats independent of the king, vehemently disagreed.

The Parlement demanded the crown cease its military expansionist policy and implement constitutional and financial reform. Mazarin responded by arresting and jailing the Parlement's most prominent members. News of the arrests led to a public uprising: Parisians shut up their shops and businesses and took to the streets. This marked the beginning of the Fronde, the civil war that took its name from a slingshot used by street children to annoy figures of authority.

The Fronde comprised two insurrections in five years: the 1648–49 Fronde de Parlement, which aimed to check the growing absolute power of the monarchy; and the 1650–53 Fronde des Nobles, a struggle for power among discontented aristocrats. The first riots, including the storming of the Palais-Royal, frightened the crown and the jailed members of the Parlement were released. However, this did not stop the riots, and Louis and his mother Anne fled the city. The insult

BELOW: Frondeurs at the 1652 Battle of the Faubourg Saint Antoine are shown trapped between the walls of the Bastille and the Porte St Antoine, one of the gates of Paris.

to the royal family would not be forgotten. Anne ordered the Prince de Condé, France's greatest military general, to storm Paris and take back control. It was to be a harder task than Condé realized.

'Paris had fallen into a familiar state of hunger, misery and lawlessness.'

Rather than march into the city and quash the uprising, Condé was forced to lay siege, just as Henri IV had done in 1590; much of the weaponry used against Condé was in fact from that era. Condé made few initial gains in Paris; after cutting off the city's water supply there was little he could do but wait. The rioting Frondeurs, on the other hand, were having rather more success and took the Bastille prison. To break the impasse, Condé offered an amnesty for the Frondeurs if they laid down their weapons. With this agreed, Louis and Anne returned to the capital.

However, in an act of treachery typical of French royalist politics then and later, Cardinal Mazarin arrested Condé. He was afraid Condé would join the side of the Frondeurs after winning Paris back for the crown; by arresting him, Mazarin made sure this actually happened. Now Condé led his men against the crown and the streets of the capital quickly came under mob rule.

Louis and Anne were put under house arrest at the Palais-Royal, a further insult that Louis would not forget; nor would he forgive the nobles responsible. For Louis, Paris, the nobles, and the common people were a crucible of lethal threats and danger; he would flee the city as soon as possible.

In fact, there was little incentive for anyone to live in Paris at that time. Paris had fallen into a familiar state of hunger, misery and lawlessness. Then, in 1652, the citizens of Paris opened the city gates to Condé and his men. They were to be quickly disappointed by this decision.

Massacre of the Hôtel de Ville

To win the city's support and establish order, Condé organized a meeting between members of the Fronde, the bourgeoisie, and the clergy in a meeting hall in the Hôtel de Ville. However, relations soured when reconciliation with the crown was suggested. Shots were fired and Condé's men attacked the meeting. Mademoiselle de Montpensier, cousin to Louis XIV, wrote in her memoirs of the ensuing massacre:

'Then the mob started shouting that they must kill and burn Mazarin, and some of the most strong and sturdy tried to break the front door of the town hall, while their riflemen and musketeers shot through the windows. But, the door being strong, they resorted to collecting straw and faggots and set fire to the front door as well as two small rooms, which were soon consumed. It started at four in the afternoon and people saw the smoke from all the ends of Paris.' (*Memoirs of Mademoiselle de Montpensier*, translated by Henry Colburn)

In the morning, a few survivors appeared from the cellar below the hall, which had been burned to the ground. The 100 or so bodies of the dead were laid in the Place de Grève to be identified.

The Massacre of the Hôtel de Ville was the final straw for the battle-weary people of Paris; it was also the end of Condé's political career. The disgraced general stole away from the city, and the Fronde folded in on itself. It was the last act of armed resistance to royal French power until the revolution of 1789. Louis was now in control, and he would spend the rest of his reign making his power absolute.

Louis made his intentions clear from the outset. He established himself at his Louvre palace, punished all members of the Fronde, and installed only loyalists in administrative positions. To celebrate the one-year anniversary of the Massacre of the Hôtel de Ville, Louis threw a party for the city and installed a statue of himself outside the city hall, a god-like figure bearing a bolt of lightning and with one foot on a ship bearing the Parisian coat of arms.

ABOVE: Louis XIV greets his loyalists from the Palais-Royal, where he was put under house arrest after returning to Paris. He would never forgive the wrongs that had been committed against his family.

OPPOSITE: The Prince de Condé was a military hero and France's best commander. He was also duplicitous, self-serving, and likely to turn his coat.

COUR DES MIRACLES

One of the no-go areas of Paris was the Cour des Miracles, a neighbourhood located by the Filles-Dieu convent that seventeenth-century historian Henry Sauval described as 'a great cul-de-sac that was stinking, muddy, irregular and unpaved… another world in one of the most poorly built and dirtiest of neighbourhoods.' The Cour des Miracles, popularly thought to be ruled by thieves, murderers and prostitutes, was so named after its beggars who would miraculously lose (or wash away) their signs of disability or disease after returning home.

Although a real neighbourhood, the myths surrounding the Cour des Miracles are today thought to have been exaggerated. This is because the Cour represented aspects of working-class Parisian life unpalatable to the bourgeoisie and royal court such as poverty, an immigrant population, and a type of urban self-governance that was independent of Louis' absolute rule. In modern times, the Cour des Miracles is sometimes used to disparage parts of Paris that are typically made up of working-class immigrants.

When Cardinal Mazarin died in 1661, Louis did not appoint a new first minister, but took over the role himself. He explained the new rules to the Parlement:

'Up to this moment I have been pleased to entrust the government of my affairs to the late Cardinal. It is now time that I govern them myself. I request and order you to seal no orders except by my command . . . I order you not to sign anything, not even a passport without my command; to render account to me personally each day and to favor no one.'

Parlement quickly learned not to do anything without the king's consent. One day while out hunting, Louis discovered the Parlement had called a meeting without his knowledge. He galloped the several miles back to Paris and burst into the Parlement chambers brandishing his riding crop, saying: 'L'etat, c'est moi' ('I am the state'). There would not be another meeting without the king's say-so.

Louis ruled from then on like a Roman emperor, and it was even suggested that he would remodel Paris into a city that would rival Rome. Paris at that time, however, was a city in tatters: murder and thievery were rife, streets and housing were dilapidated, and there was little to eat. It was also dangerous to go outside: more than 350 people were killed on the streets of Paris in 1643 alone. In 1665, the head of the city's police force, the Lieutenant Criminal, was murdered alongside his wife.

The New City

To combat its criminal element and create a city worthy of his reign, Louis and his newly appointed Controller-General of Finances, Jean-Baptiste Colbert, began planning Paris' rejuvenation. He removed the medieval city walls built by Philippe Auguste, making the city a more open space. The aim was to remove undesirables and gentrify the city. To do this, the new head of the police, the Lieutenant-Général de Police, was ordered to round up beggars, prostitutes and criminals and deliver them elsewhere. This often meant being shipped to the Hôpital General, a hospital originally built for plague victims, which under Louis became a dumping

OPPOSITE: A scene from the legendary Cour des Miracles, a stinking cul-de-sac where thieves and murderers were a law unto themselves.

L'AFFAIRE DES POISONS

The so-called Affair of the Poisons, a murder investigation that saw members of Louis' court sentenced on charges of murder and witchcraft, was the great scandal of the age. It began with the 1676 trial of Madame de Brinvilliers, who, along with her lover, was found guilty of poisoning her father and two brothers to inherit their estates. De Brinvilliers had confessed to these crimes under the torture of a water cure, which involved filling a victim's body with water. She was then beheaded and burned at the stake.

The trial appeared to expose a circle of prisoners, fortune-tellers and alchemists, who were accused of selling poison and aphrodisiacs to a number of French nobles. The most prominent of the accused was Catherine Monvoisin, nicknamed 'La Voisin', who implicated several members of Louis XIV's inner circle including his mistress Madame de Montespan. De Montespan was accused of several crimes, including attempting to poison her rival Marie-Angélique de Fontanges, feeding the king aphrodisiacs, and participating in black magic rituals to secure his affections.

La Voisin's accomplice, a priest called Étienne Guibourg, confirmed the accusations against de Montespan. Physically deformed and blind in one eye, Guibourg described a black mass where the devil was invoked by placing a crucifix on a naked woman's

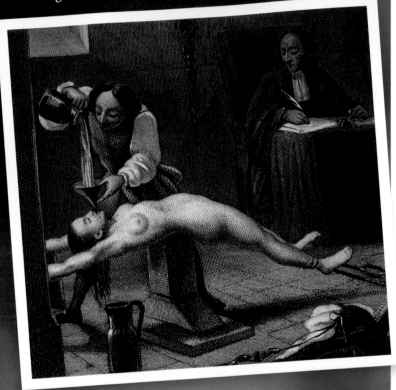

BELOW: Madame de Brinvilliers is tortured by having her stomach filled to capacity with water. She eventually confessed to her alleged crimes.

belly. He also reported the slaughter and disembowelling of an infant, whose blood, viscera and ground-up bones were used in a potion fed to Louis by de Montespan.

Whatever the realities were behind the accusations, Louis was not going to allow his mistress of 17 years, who had borne him several bastards, to be burned at the stake. He ordered de Montespan to be acquitted. She stayed at court for a short time before being exiled to a convent for the last 17 years of her life. In 1682, La Voisin and 32 others were burned at the stake for witchcraft, which brought the affair to an end.

ground for anyone considered socially objectionable. By 1700, over 10,000 paupers were estimated to be crammed into the Hôpital alone.

Next Louis ordered grand works that included the Observatory; the Invalides veteran hospital; new façades for the Louvre and Tuileries palaces; a number of wide boulevards to enable the passage of carriages; along with several triumphal arches, public fountains and more than 6000 street lamps. This did not mean Louis had become a friend of Paris. He loathed the Paris city council, viewed the Parlement with a suspicion bordering on paranoia, and was bewildered by the apparent inability of Parisians to love him unconditionally. The king appealed to the city's great Catholic majority in his 1685 revocation of the Edict of Nantes, which would lead to great persecution of Protestants, but nothing seemed to work. In 1666, following the death of his mother Anne, Louis began the move to his new Palace of Versailles.

Paris to Versailles

The Affair of the Poisons symbolized the end of Louis' tenure in Paris. In 1682, he moved permanently to his new palace at Versailles and visited his capital a few dozen times more over the next 44 years of his life. The king's life at Versailles, however, would have a great effect on his capital city, not only during his reign, but also in the 100 years following it. For the Versailles years were when Louis established his absolute authority over the French nobility, church and bourgeoisie, and the nation as a whole. Under Louis, France became one of the great European superpowers, and he alone was responsible for every decision. The

ABOVE: Louis XIV and his court enjoy the Grotte de Thétys in the extensive grounds at Versailles. The palace gardens covered 800 landscaped hectares, and their design occupied much of Louis' time.

ABOVE: Louis XIV sits among his favourite courtiers dressed in the *Justaucorps à brevet*, a blue silk jacket reserved for 50 of the most privileged nobles.

exploited Third Estate suffered most. These were citizens who were neither clergy nor nobility and were the only members of French society to pay tax. This tax provided Louis and his hundreds of courtiers with every imaginable extravagance; his people went without. However, the Third Estate would get its revenge in 1789, when it rose up against the monarchy.

Louis' exodus to Versailles, around 20km (12 miles) southwest of Paris, was part of his wider plan to control the nobles. Louis had 350 apartments built in the vast palace for his royal court. Every aspect of this royal life at Versailles was intricately choreographed. Disobedience meant the end of royal favours and, in extreme cases, exile and death. Louis had constructed Versailles as a gilded cage where he could control every aspect of his nobles' lives. He would keep them occupied with extravagant banquets, balls, hunting trips, and theatrical productions, and in return, the courtiers would surrender their freedom to him.

Dressing for Court

Louis controlled everything down to the smallest details of the nobles' wardrobe. The proper dress, Louis said, would 'encourage loyalty, satisfy vanity, impress the outside world.' He led by example, wearing a wig, white hosiery and encouraging the wearing of red heels to symbolize 'the elevation of his court above the rest of humanity.' The most valuable item of clothing was the *Justaucorps à brevet*, a blue silk jacket embroidered in silver and gold that only 50 courtiers were allowed to wear. When one of these courtiers died, the jacket was a valued inheritance that could be passed to another.

Louis required that each courtier had a different outfit for every formal event, meaning that courtiers had to spend huge amounts. Usually these clothes not only showed off the wearer's wealth, but were extremely uncomfortable, impractical and difficult to maintain. Generally, the cost of an outfit was determined by the amount of cloth it used, but smaller items made of lace could be prohibitively expensive. A lace cravat for a nobleman, for example, would have the equivalent cost today of a luxury sports car or even a small yacht. As a result, many courtiers fell into debt trying to remain fashionable and had to ask Louis for loans to buy new clothes. This ensured that nobles at Versailles were kept too poor and preoccupied at court to contemplate rebellion.

At Versailles, every aspect of the king's life was a public performance. The greatest honour was being allowed to be present at Louis' 7.30 a.m. *petit levée*, or morning rising ceremony. This began with an examination by the king's doctors, a group visit to the royal commode, and the helping on of the king's shirt – the greatest privilege of all. After a light breakfast, Louis took mass in his chapel, where the wider throng of courtiers that did not make up his immediate retinue gathered around trying to be noticed.

Louis would lunch at noon, watched over by a group of standing courtiers, and then hold a lavish ceremonial dinner in the evening. Here, the dining room mirrored the complicated hierarchy of the court, where family members and those in favour could sit and join in, while other less privileged members were invited to participate by standing and observing. In the evening, Louis' bedtime rituals emulated those of the morning, with eager favourites competing for the honour of holding the royal candlestick.

'Every aspect of royal life at Versailles was intricately choreographed.'

BELOW: Breakfasting with Louis XIV was a great honour bestowed upon only a very few at Versailles. Here, the king shares his table with the playwright Molière.

To survive at Versailles, every courtier had to understand the unwritten minutiae of courtly etiquette and follow them religiously – hats had to be removed when the king passed; only princes and princesses could sit next to him. Everything about the courtiers' lives was dictated by the king: what they wore, what they did, and where they stood on the social ladder. Those at the top would be granted land, favours, titles, and the sexual attention of those wishing to climb. In this environment, vices were tolerated, but a faux pas could ruin a courtier's life. At lower levels, Versailles meant a cramped, claustrophobic existence, where a courtier could quietly go bankrupt while making up the numbers and being completely ignored.

Louis encouraged vanity, sexual intrigue, and other pursuits that would distract the nobles' attention from the brutalities of his reign. Behind the scenes, he monitored all aspects of life at Versailles, from the latest sex scandal to the gossip of servants; his spies intercepted the nobles' letters. The authors of any seditious murmurings were dispatched swiftly and without fuss.

Maintaining an artificial universe at Versailles, with the Sun King at its celestial centre, cost a fortune. Although France became wealthy under Louis, he nearly bankrupted it in the end. Domestically, he placed heavy restrictions on workers to keep them under the thumb, discouraged industrial inventiveness, and introduced unreasonably high tariffs on trade. His revocation of the Edict of Nantes, and the persecutions that followed, led 200,000 of the country's

BELOW: A renewed round of Huguenot persecution began in 1685 after Louis' revocation of the Edict of Nantes. Over 200,000 Huguenots fled the country at this time, many of them to England.

By the end of his 72-year-reign, Louis had all but bankrupted the country. His tax on every individual in France added to the suffering. The days of an absolute monarch were now numbered.

highly skilled Huguenot artisans and business owners to flee the country.

To increase revenue, Louis introduced the 'capitation', a tax on every person, including the clergy and nobles, which was considered an unthinkable affront. However, it was not enough to pay Louis' costs: by his death in 1715 France was 1.1 trillion *livres* in debt. By then, rolling crop failures and rising food prices had prompted many peasants to raid grain stores to feed themselves. As a symbol of solidarity, Louis melted down some of his gold plates, but his excesses at court continued unabated.

This was the model that remained after Louis died: a country ruled over by a despot who lived in luxury with the nobles while the people suffered. His failure to provide institutions to distribute the country's wealth fairly, or to enact a democratic parliament that would speak for those without wealth or privilege, led to generations of impoverished, disaffected Frenchmen. Their chance to speak out would come in 1789, during the greatest and bloodiest insurrection ever to sweep France. Louis, however, would take his final leave with a last immortal line: '*Je m'envais, mais l'État demeurera toujours*' ('I depart, but the State shall always remain').

The French Revolution

The wedding between Louis-Auguste, soon to be Louis XV, and his 14-year-old bride Marie Antoinette, was considered by many as a terrible portent. During the festivities, a fireworks display in the Place de la Concorde went horribly wrong. A rogue skyrocket set a box of fireworks alight and a fire swept through the square; 132 died in the ensuing melee. In two decades' time, more French lives would be lost in the Place de la Concorde, although this time it would be before an inflamed crowd baying for blood.

> '**To wear longer trousers was the most visible sign of social inferiority.**'

The gap between Paris' rich and poor had never been as wide as in the eighteenth century. When not at Versailles, Parisian nobles spent their time entertaining, visiting the theatre, and adopting new fads and affectations. The carrying of parasols and *pantins* became in vogue from the 1760s, the latter describing a small puppet that could be played with while idling on the Pont Neuf. The wearing of wigs, the carrying of handkerchiefs and snuffboxes, and the adoption of foppish, effeminate airs were designed to contrast with the habits and clothes of the commoners, known as the *sans-culottes*. Culottes were the fashionable above-the-knee breeches of the nobility; to wear longer trousers was the most visible sign of social inferiority.

Adventurous aristocrats would dress down to visit the cramped, working-class faubourgs of Paris; those who lived there were considered no better than the dangerous savages being discovered abroad in distant colonies. Many working-class Parisians were actually immigrants from the provinces, who had moved to Paris to fill the vacancies left by the city's high mortality rate.

Those Parisians who did not die on a foreign battlefield, or from smallpox, often succumbed to the many other diseases that thrived in insanitary and crowded houses. Venereal disease was rife: syphilis at that time was an excruciating and incurable disease that many babies were born with, a product of Parisian prostitution. A conservative estimate of the city's prostitutes in 1760 is around 20,000, although the true number of those involved in casual sex for payment was certainly higher.

OPPOSITE: Parisian prostitutes are rounded up for imprisonment in the Hospice de la Salpêtrière, a city hospital that became a dumping ground for undesirables. Many Salpêtrière internees were released during the September massacres.

ABOVE: Nobles show off Parisian fashion circa 1760. Culottes were the above-the-knee breeches favoured by the aristocracy. The 'sans-culottes' were commoners who often wore their trousers long as a badge of working-class pride.

There was little provision in Paris for the suffering working class. The city's main hospital was the Hôtel-Dieu, which crammed six people to a bed and had a mortality rate of one in four. However, new ideas about hygiene and sanitation were beginning to inform the policy of city planners; it became less acceptable to tip household faeces and urine into the street; the dead began to be buried outside the city centre. Smaller hospitals were opened that aimed to heal the sick rather than simply admitting them.

There were new ideas about politics too, a product of Enlightenment ideals that were gaining increasing support among the middle class. The bourgeoisie were ambitious and well read, schooled in the theories of Montesquieu, Rousseau and Voltaire and other Enlightenment thinkers known as the 'philosophes'. The philosophes believed that social, economic and political reform was necessary to overhaul France's outdated feudal institutions and create a state that represented the will of its people. Human beings had certain natural rights and were entitled to freedom, happiness and knowledge.

The spread of Enlightenment ideas was encouraged among middle-class 'societies of thought', such as reading rooms, coffee houses, Masonic lodges, and scientific academies. It was here that the great bourgeois slogan was born of liberty, equality and fraternity.

While the middle class sought political power, however, there was no central philosophy underpinning the French revolution, nor was there one unified party leading the charge. Instead there was a broad desire from both the bourgeoisie and peasantry of the Third Estate for greater representation in government and full land-owning rights. Without an economic and political crisis it is uncertain if the Third Estate would have risen. But in the late 1780s, this crisis came, when France was crippled by debt, poor harvests, and a monarch who had bankrupted the country.

Shots are Fired

In 1789, an unsettled climate of dissatisfaction and frustration hung heavily over France. In response to calls for a fairer tax system, in June Louis XVI summoned the Estates-General, a government assembly that had not met for more than 200 years. This desperate measure resulted in representatives of the Third Estate occupying a Versailles tennis court and refusing to disperse until Louis recognized them as a new National Constituent Assembly. The Declaration of the Rights of Man and of the Citizen would become this new government's manifesto against absolute monarchy and the rule of nobles.

On 20 June 1789, when the Third Estate declared itself the new Parlement, it seemed like anything was possible. But, by July, desperation and anger had once again set in. Louis reacted to the uprising by bolstering his military presence around Paris and Versailles. Political rage was boosted by increasing food shortages. Hungry peasants, unemployed workers, and other members of the disaffected masses swarmed onto the streets of Paris. Unbeknown to the king, these masses were forming a people's army; when Louis removed his chancellor, the popular Jacques Necker, the army marched on Versailles. However, the protest

BELOW: Here, Third Estate representatives occupying the Versailles tennis court make an oath promising not to separate until a constitution for France has been established.

was peaceful and called only for Necker to be reinstated. Louis ignored the calls and in so doing sparked the powder keg that set the revolution alight.

On 14 July, an angry mob stormed the Invalides barracks and armed themselves with the weapons they found there. Bristling with pikes, muskets and swords, the crowd famously marched to the Bastille prison, a hated symbol of royal authority. The prison governor tried reasoning with the crowd. When this failed, he ordered his men to fire; more than 100 people were killed. The mob responded with murderous rage, storming the prison wall and freeing its seven prisoners; they burned the Bastille to the ground, seized the prison governor, sheared off his head and stuck it on a pike.

'Is this a rebellion?' 'No, sire,' came the reply, 'it is a revolution.'

A wave of violence swept Paris: the convent at Roi Soleil was sacked; buildings at the Hôtel de Ville destroyed; and various figures of hate were decapitated and had their heads put on display. Louis, believing he had done enough to satisfy the mob, was genuinely surprised at the news from Paris. Returning to Versailles

THE DECLARATION OF THE RIGHTS OF MAN

Written by the liberal French aristocrat, the Marquis de Lafayette, with help from Thomas Jefferson, in Paris at the time, the Declaration stated that all men are born free, equal before the law and have natural rights to property, life and liberty. The government's proper role was to recognize and secure the rights and property of its citizens, and it would be formed by elected, tax-paying citizens. Women, slaves and foreigners were not included. However, the sentiment behind the Declaration would inform the French abolition of slavery in 1794; Britain and America would follow in 1807 and 1808 respectively. A key principle of the Declaration – that 'All human beings are born free and equal in dignity and rights' – lived on to became the first article in the 1948 Universal Declaration of Human Rights.

LEFT: An engraving of The Declaration of the Rights of Man and of the Citizen.

after a day's hunt, the king asked one of his aides, 'Is this a rebellion?' 'No, sire,' came the reply, 'it is a revolution.'

Fearing that Versailles would be stormed and the royal family massacred, Louis made his way to Paris. His outward appearance suggested he had accepted the will of the people and wanted to renegotiate his royal powers. Some believe the kind Louis intended to reinvent his role as the loved 'Father of France' figure, Henri IV. However, in reality Louis was simply stalling for time. Many of his nobles fled to neighbouring countries such as Prussia to try to drum up support for the monarch. Louis dressed in sombre black and took a plain carriage to Paris, where he was given a cockade featuring the red, white and blue colours of the revolution, and addressed the crowd. His tone was conciliatory and meek, and was met with cheers and cannon fire. When he returned to Versailles, his reign, and the *ancien régime*, were all but finished.

ABOVE: Jacques Necker was a popular politician whose suggested social reforms included the creation of a constitutional monarchy based on the English model. His proposals were rejected by the king.

The Women's March

Parisians were wrong if they imagined the recent revolutionary events and Louis' apparent capitulation would improve their quality of life. By October 1789, inflation was high and the cost of living prohibitive. The cost of a loaf of bread was worth a worker's entire daily income; violence broke out in the marketplaces. Matters were made worse by reports that during a drunken banquet Versailles soldiers had trampled on the new revolutionary tricolour flag. Any good feeling that existed between Versailles and the people of Paris evaporated when Louis made a statement agreeing to only some of the decrees of the new French constitution while also expressing doubts about the Declaration of the Rights of Man.

The tipping point came on the morning of 5 October, when a group of market women, infuriated at the price of food, armed themselves with kitchen knives and other makeshift weaponry and stormed the Hôtel de Ville, seizing its store of food, arms and other provisions. Then the crowd, now numbering several thousand, marched on Versailles. The city's national guard, led by popular war hero the Marquis de Lafayette, had little choice but to escort the women, try to calm them down, and hope for the best.

By the time the women had walked the 20km (12 miles) through driving rain from Paris to Versailles they were exhausted. The marchers appeared, however, to

Here the governor of the Bastille, Bernard-René de Launay tries to reason with the revolutionary mob. He was subsequently arrested, decapitated, and had his head stuck on a pike.

LOUIS ENTERS PARIS

ABOVE: Louis XVI is received by Jean Sylvain Bailly, a leader of the Revolution. Bailly was later guillotined during the Reign of Terror.

American founding father Thomas Jefferson was in Paris working as a diplomat during the French Revolution and described Louis' trip to Paris in a letter:

'The king came to Paris, leaving the queen in consternation for his return… the king's carriage was in the center, on each side of it the States general, in two ranks, afoot, at their head the Marquis de la Fayette as commander-in-chief, on horseback, and Bourgeois guards before and behind. About 60,000 citizens of all forms and colours, armed with the muskets of the Bastille and Invalids as far as they would go, the rest with pistols, swords, pikes, pruning hooks, scythes, lined all the streets thro' which the procession passed, and, with the crowds of people in the streets, doors and windows, saluted them every where with cries of "vive la nation." But not a single "vive le roi" was heard.

'The king landed at the Hôtel de Ville. There, Monsieur Bailly presented and put into his hat the popular cockade, and addressed him. The king being unprepared and unable to answer, Bailly went to him, gathered from him some scraps of sentences, and made out an answer, which he delivered to the audience as from their king. On their return, the popular cries were "vive le roi et la nation." He was conducted by a Garde Bourgeoise to his palace at Versailles … Tranquility is now restored to the capital; the shops are again opened; the people resuming their labors.' (Thomas Jefferson, *Letter to John Jay*)

be simply protesting about the lack of food. Some of the women were granted an audience with the king, who appeared sympathetic, and gave food to the crowd. This was enough for some of the marchers, who trooped back towards Paris. A larger section of the crowd, however, remained unpacified and continued to occupy the grounds of the Palace.

Alarmed by the hostility of the mob, Louis immediately volunteered to agree to every decree of the new constitution and to ratify the Declaration of the Rights of Man. Believing this would disperse the crowd, the king went to bed, as did Lafayette. Lafayette's soldiers, on the other hand, stayed to mingle with the protesters outside. By morning, many of these soldiers had joined the rebellion.

At around 6 a.m. the protesters found an unguarded door into the Palace and stormed inside. The king's Swiss Guard tried to barricade the interior doors and even shot one of the protesters, but were quickly overcome. Those who fought back suffered the new revolutionary punishment of decapitation, and had their heads lifted atop pikes. Marie Antoinette and her ladies-in-waiting tried in vain to enter the king's bedchamber, and only passed through as the protesters broke into sight. Lafayette himself, roused from a few hours of sleep, managed to head the protesters off at Louis' bedchamber and then cleared the palace.

To calm the crowd, Lafayette convinced the king and then Marie Antoinette to greet the protesters from the safety of a balcony. Lafayette even attached a tricolour cockade to one of the king's servants to help matters along. The scene on the balcony was an extraordinary piece of theatre that saved the royal family. The king called for calm, and Lafayette tenderly knelt before the queen and kissed her hand. This seemed to soften the demonstrators' anger: they agreed to vacate the palace on condition that the royal family came with them to Paris.

BELOW: By the time the protestors of the Women's March had walked the 20km (12 miles) through the driving rain to Versailles they were exhausted. However, they would not leave without the king.

So the marching crowd provided an escort for the king's carriage. It was a rowdy journey with muskets fired in celebration and the heads of the slain held high on pikes. There was now no question of who was in charge: the king and queen were at the service of the people. When they reached the Tuileries, now a prison for the royals, they found the palace in a state of disrepair. Louis commented that it was 'far from providing the comforts to which His Majesty was accustomed in other royal residences.' He told his large entourage to sleep where they liked and then asked that a book on the deposed English king Charles I be brought to his bedchamber.

The Tide Turns

The last roll of the dice for Louis came on 20 June 1791. Stealing away through secret passages beneath the Tuileries, the king, his family and entourage fled Paris. The plan was to cross the border and mount a counter-revolution with the 10,000 royalist troops stationed at the French frontier town of Montmédy. To stay close to his family, Louis dismissed two small, fast carriages for a large, slow model that creaked under the weight of the royals and their extensive luggage. This, combined with multiple rest stops during which the royal family chatted with passers-by, was a fatal error. The carriage was identified and stopped at the small town of Varennes, 50km (31 miles) from Montmédy. Louis was taken back to Paris under a revolutionary armed guard.

Perhaps surprisingly, Louis' carriage was not greeted by a loud, angry mob as it trundled through the streets of Paris back to the Tuileries, but an eerie silence. The overriding feeling among the throng was of shock: their king had betrayed

BELOW: Louis XVI is arrested at Varennes after fleeing Paris. By chatting with passers-by, stopping for multiple rest-stops and employing a large, slow carriage, the royal family virtually sabotaged their own escape.

them. The National Constituent Assembly, now the ruling power of France, suggested that Louis could remain king if he signed the constitution. However, a vitriolic letter left by Louis at the Tuileries for the revolutionaries to find showed his true intentions. Louis outlined the indignities suffered by himself and his family, admitted that his oath to the constitution had been insincere and called for a return to the monarchy. The letter exposed the king's duplicity and ended any chance of a royal reconciliation with the people.

The problem for Louis was that his escape had opened up warring factions within the Assembly. These factions soon became political 'clubs' with names such as the Jacobins and Cordeliers. Some called for a fully democratic republic without a king; others wanted a constitutional monarchy. There was also disagreement within the clubs themselves: the Jacobins, for instance, were split into the moderate 'Girondins' and radical 'Montagnards'.

The conflicting views of the Assembly were unpopular with the people of Paris, who worried that it was becoming weak and ineffective. On 17 July 1791, two days after the Assembly issued a decree that Louis would remain king under a constitutional monarchy, 50,000 Parisians took to the streets in protest.

Many of the protesters had been roused by the Cordeliers, who sought signatures for their petition calling for Louis' abdication. The petition was displayed at the Champ de Mars, but when the protesters arrived a scuffle broke out with the National Guard there. Unbeknown to the crowd, the Mayor of Paris, Jean Sylvain Bailly, had ordered the guard to disperse the crowd. After stones were thrown, the head of the guards, the Marquis de Lafayette, ordered them to shoot into the crowd. Bayonets were fixed and a police riot ensued.

ABOVE: Revolutionary leader and Mayor of Paris, Jean Sylvain Bailly mounts the guillotine scaffold. He was reportedly asked 'Do you tremble, Bailly?' He answered, 'Yes, but it is only the cold.'

ABOVE: Louis XVI under house arrest at the Tuileries Palace. Up until the end he hoped that a foreign power would intervene to save him and the French monarchy. His fate, however, was sealed.

Between 12 and 100 people died at the so-called Massacre of the Champ de Mars. Eyewitnesses reported that the number was low because the guard, mainly made up of citizen volunteers, were generally bad shots and also unwilling to inflict bodily harm. However, the damage between the National Guard and the people was done; Lafayette's reputation was shattered. Bailly was sent to the guillotine by the Legislative Assembly, the new government that had replaced the National Constituent Assembly. Bailly, one of the original heroes of the revolution, was the first of many heads to roll under the charge of anti-revolutionary behaviour.

It was the job of the Legislative Assembly to carry forward the ideals of the revolution as the first constitutional government of France. The king's part in this government remained unclear; Louis himself was still under house arrest in the Tuileries.

Louis had secretly hoped a foreign power would intervene to save him and the monarchy. This looked a distinct possibility; in 1792 France went to war against both Austria and Prussia. Marie Antoinette had been a pivotal figure in bringing about the war, convincing her brother, the Holy Roman Emperor Leopold II, to invade France and reinstate the monarchy. This had two important results. The first was a wave of nationalism, which resulted in large numbers of Frenchmen joining the revolutionary army. The second was a pre-emptive strike, called by a new radical Paris Commune, the city government, and the well-known revolutionary journalist, Jean-Paul Marat. Marat argued that jailed members of the aristocracy should be dealt with before a foreign power could free them. The Commune then mobilized a crowd of insurgents to storm the Tuileries and massacre the Swiss Guard protecting the king.

Next, the Commune imprisoned the royal family in the Temple fortress and drew up a list of 'opponents of the Revolution', sealing the gates to the city. Nobles' houses were raided and hundreds thrown in prison. Finally, the Commune ordered the September massacres, the wholesale slaughter of 2000 prisoners considered enemies of the state, including 200 Catholic priests.

The violence was not confined to Paris, as copycat massacres of nobles and priests spread across France. Chaos persisted until a new Assembly, the National Convention, was convened to restore order. This happened to coincide with a defeat of Prussian forces at Valmy. Bolstered by the good news, the Convention's first act was to abolish the monarchy and proclaim France a republic.

War and internecine fighting among moderate Girondins and radical Montagnards meant the Convention gave way in 1793 to the notorious Committee of Public Safety. A Montagnard group led by the infamous revolutionary Pierre Robespierre, the committee was given dictatorial powers to deal with counter-revolutionary crimes, to prosecute dissenters, and deliver the 'Terror' to France. The Committee, in conjunction with its judicial body the Revolutionary Tribunal, would commit tens of thousands to death by guillotine between September 1793 and July 1794.

The Royal End

The Terror began in earnest with the execution of Louis XVI and Marie Antoinette. Louis, charged with high treason, died on 21 January 1793. After a final morning prayer, he was transported in a covered carriage through the cold and foggy streets of Paris to the Place de la Revolution – now known as Place de la Concorde. There, national guardsmen stood four deep around the guillotine, following reports of a planned rescue of the king. A scuffle did take place a few blocks away, but was quickly put down by the guardsmen. At 10 a.m., Louis mounted the scaffold and had his hands tied. His executioner,

THE SEPTEMBER MASSACRES

The massacres in Paris electrified Europe: supporters of the status quo and liberal reformers alike were appalled at the killings. Newspapers compared the massacre to the sacking of Rome and reported acts of cannibalism, hearts being ripped from live bodies and revolutionaries dipping their bread into their victims' blood. Other, more plausible, eyewitness accounts were only slightly less lurid, as details emerged of an orgy of bloodshed. This is how *The Times* of London reported the killing of the Princess de Lamballe, a favourite of Marie Antoinette:

'When the mob went to the prison de la Force, where the Royal attendants were chiefly confined, the Princess De Lamballe went down on her knees to implore a suspension of her fate for 24 hours. This was at first granted, until a second mob more ferocious than the first, forced her apartments, and decapitated her. The circumstances which attended her death were such as makes humanity shudder, and which decency forbids us to repeat:—Previous to her death, the mob offered her every insult. Her thighs were cut

ABOVE: Princess de Lamballe is seized by the crowd before being brutally executed in a frenzy of savagery.

across, and her bowels and heart torn from her, and for two days her mangled body was dragged through the streets.' (*The Times*, 10 September 1792)

Henri Sanson, recounted the following moments in his memoirs:

'The King held out his hands, while his confessor was presenting a crucifix to his lips. Two assistants tied the hands which had wielded a sceptre. He then ascended the steps of the scaffold, supported by the worthy priest. "Are these drums going to sound for ever?" he said. On reaching the platform, he advanced to the side where the crowd was the thickest, and made such an imperative sign that the drummers stopped for a moment. "Frenchmen!" he exclaimed, in a strong voice, "you see your King ready to die for you. May my blood cement your happiness! I die innocent of what I am charged with!" He was about to continue when Santerre, who was at the head of his staff, ordered the drummers to beat, and nothing more could be heard. In a moment he was bound to the weigh-plank, and a few seconds afterwards, while under my touch the knife was sliding down, he could still hear the voice of the priest pronouncing these words: "Son of Saint-Louis, ascend to Heaven!" … when Gros, my assistant, showed the King's head to the multitude some cries of triumph were uttered; the greater part of the crowd turned away with profound horror.' (*Memoirs of the Sansons*, published by Chatto and Windus, 1876)

There were reports that Louis' head blinked or even cried out upon falling into the basket below the guillotine. What is certainly known is the great amount of blood the execution produced; it reportedly spurted from Louis' neck as the executioner's aides collected his body. Some spectators ran forward to dip their handkerchiefs in the blood; others even tasted it. Locks of hair, which according to tradition were the executioner's to sell, were eagerly bought up, as were items of the king's clothes. The body was then taken to an open pit,

BELOW: Louis XVI stands before his fate at the scaffold. With his beheading came the end of the absolute monarchy that began over 100 years before with the Sun King Louis XIV.

ABOVE: The show-trial of Marie-Antoinette included lurid details about her sexual deviancy, penchant for assassinating dissenters, and incest with her son. The queen took offence at the last accusation.

where it was covered with quicklime, Louis' head laid at his feet. The absolute monarchy, the blueprint for which had been laid out by Louis XIV at Versailles more than 100 years before, was no more. The Republic of France, a sovereign state run by the people, had begun.

Marie Antoinette's hearing in court, which took place nine months after Louis' execution, was typical of the show trials held by the Revolutionary Tribunal. In front of a packed courthouse, Marie Antoinette was described by the prosecution as 'the scourge and the blood-sucker of the French', a sexual deviant who had known sexual liaisons with the king's brother and even committed incest with her own son.

A stream of eyewitnesses then took the stand to denounce the queen: she had convinced Louis to appoint 'perverse' ministers; she had kept a pair of pistols in her skirts to assassinate noble dissenters; she had arranged orgies at Versailles; she had damaged her son's testicles teaching him to masturbate. The lurid testimonies were so popular with the crowd that the actual evidence against Marie Antoinette – which included letters giving away French military secrets – were all but forgotten in the uproar.

The trial created the blueprint for every subsequent case held by the Revolutionary Tribunal. From then on, so-called conspirators against the state would be sentenced to death on the flimsiest pretexts. Marie Antoinette herself was found guilty of conspiracy and intelligence with the enemy, and sentenced to the guillotine. Clothed in a white dress with her hair shorn, Marie Antoinette was transported in an open cart to the scaffold, her hands tied behind her back and tethered by a rope. The crowd jeered and threw insults as she made the hour-long

Marie-Antoinette's head is shown to the crowd. Before her execution, the queen was shorn, dressed in a plain white dress, and had her hands bound behind her back. Her body was thrown into an unmarked grave.

ABOVE: A meeting of the Committee of Public Safety led by Maximilien Robespierre. During the Committee's Reign of Terror, hundreds were sent to the guillotine every week.

journey from the Conciergerie to the Place de la Revolution. Her last words were alleged to be 'pardon me sir, I did not mean to do it,' when she stepped on executioner Henri Sanson's foot. The blade came down at 12.15 p.m.

The Terror

With the monarchy gone, the Committee of Public Safety carried out massive purges of its enemies in Paris and across France. But who were the enemies of the Republic of France? The most obvious enemies were the foreign powers at war with France; these were a very real threat to the new and vulnerable sovereign state. France, however, was also at war with itself: a revolt against the new government had broken out in the Vendée, and smaller rebellions sprang up in other regions. The Catholic Church was considered an enemy for its close alignment with the *ancien régime*. The Committee called for dechristianization. In Paris, religious processions were banned, church bells were melted down to make cannons, and cathedrals, churches and seminaries became public buildings and warehouses. Notre Dame became the 'Temple of Reason', and its statues of French kings were beheaded. Then there were the other, more obscure, enemies known only to the Committee of Public Safety. The committee deliberately used terror as a political tactic. 'Let us be terrible in order to stop the people from being so,' warned Georges Danton, reminding his fellow Committee members of the anarchy of the September Massacres.

For Maximilien Robespierre, a former lawyer and champion of the poor, terror was a necessary evil in creating a sovereign state of virtue. Robespierre's scripture for this was Enlightenment philosopher Jean-Jacques Rousseau's *Social Contract*. In this work, which hardly left Robespierre's side, Rousseau argued that an increase in liberty would lead to an increase in virtue. Now that liberty had been achieved by the revolutionaries, Robespierre believed that virtue must follow, whatever the human cost.

'If the basis of popular government in peacetime is virtue, the basis of popular government during a revolution is both virtue and terror; virtue, without which terror is baneful; terror, without which virtue is powerless. Terror is nothing more than speedy, severe and inflexible justice; it is thus an emanation of virtue; it is less a principle in itself, than a consequence of the general principle of democracy.'

(Maximilien Robespierre, *Report upon the Principles of Political Morality*, translated by B. Bache)

The committee issued a decree outlining its strategy: 'It [the Committee] firmly intends to be terrible towards its enemies, generous towards its allies, and just towards its peoples.' But what followed was the creation of a totalitarian police state that filled the prisons to bursting point and found thousands guilty of treason without legitimate trials or examination of evidence. Each week hundreds were taken in open carts from the prisons to the guillotine. So many were killed that it was feared the blood-soaked ground beneath the guillotine would pollute the water supply.

As the terror increased, the Committee passed the Law of Suspects, a decree that eliminated almost all individual freedoms and rights. The law allowed the arrest of not only 'enemies' of the revolution, but also 'likely enemies' and the burden of proof was now on the suspects to prove their innocence. Parisians were made to carry 'certificates of civism' to prove their revolutionary loyalties. Widespread covert surveillance of the public began; an army of undercover police officers arrested anyone under the slightest pretext. Paranoia gripped the capital: no one knew if they were being watched, or about to be accused of some wrongdoing.

The Law of Suspects, however, was only a prelude; it was followed by the infamous Law of 22 Prairial, also known as the 'Law of the Great Terror'. This simplified all aspects of the indictment and prosecution of political criminals, who the Committee argued were more injurious to the state than common criminals. In its simplest terms, the Law of 22 Prairial allowed the arrest of suspects for any reason and stripped away every legal right of defence. As Committee member Georges Couthon explained, 'For a citizen to become suspect it is sufficient that rumour accuses him'.

A trial held under Law of 22 Prairial therefore consisted of the accused defending themselves, as no defence counsel was allowed, and a jury coming to a verdict of acquittal or death. The most terrifying aspect of the Law of 22 Prairial was its introduction of the concept of thought crimes: state prosecutors were instructed to decipher people's faces and read their minds for signs of dissent. Juries were told to commit defendants on instinct. The Committee justified these ideas by saying that virtuous defendants would reveal no fear in their faces.

Hundreds were summarily executed with the barest semblance of a trial. Lists of the accused began to fill the filing cabinets of the police,

BELOW: A Committee of Public Safety warrant for the arrest of Georges Danton, an early leader of the Revolution and one-time member of the Committee.

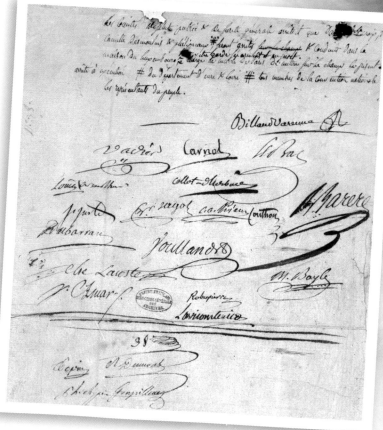

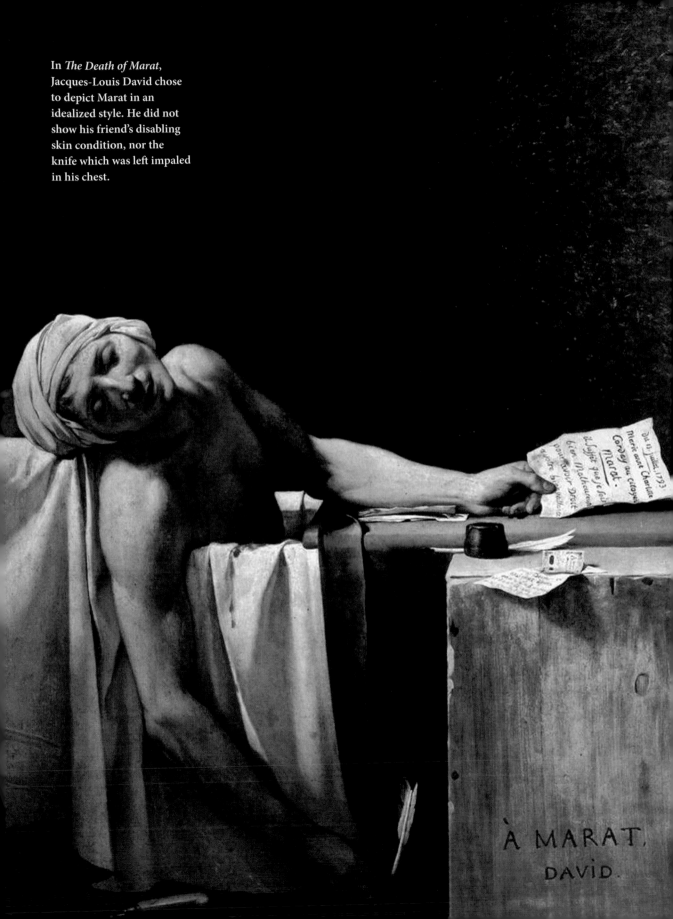

In *The Death of Marat*, Jacques-Louis David chose to depict Marat in an idealized style. He did not show his friend's disabling skin condition, nor the knife which was left impaled in his chest.

À MARAT.

DAVID.

a growing bureaucracy serviced by spies. Robespierre, who had once been an opponent of capital punishment, now had his own police bureau, where he and his staff sifted through endless denunciations in their hunt for enemies of the state.

Robespierre himself was becoming increasingly paranoid, fearing there was no one left he could trust. As the work of the Committee went on, more and more allies of the revolution were condemned to death. Most shockingly, those executed included the revolutionary stalwarts Camille Desmoulins, Robespierre's school friend, and Georges Danton, an original member of the Committee of Public Safety.

Desmoulins' crime had been to call for an end to terror in his newspaper *Le Vieux Cordelier* ('The Old Cordelier'); Danton stood accused of financial misdeeds. Their trial, of course, was a farce. Under The Law of 22 Prairial, neither man could defend himself, and the evidence against them was simply made up. The prosecutors made clear to the jury, under a thinly veiled threat of violence, what sentence was expected of them.

> **'More and more allies of the revolution were condemned to death.'**

As Danton, Desmoulins and 14 of their accomplices mounted the guillotine scaffold, Danton uttered some last prophetic words: 'I leave it all in a frightful welter. Not a man of them has an idea of government. Robespierre will follow me; he is dragged down by me.'

According to legend, Robespierre left the shutters to his window closed on the day of the Danton and Desmoulins executions. Perhaps Robespierre felt a pang of conscience, but this did not stop him from sending many more to the guillotine. Robespierre's cult of death took the form of a religion, as he made clear in a decree in June 1794:

'The day forever fortunate has arrived, which the French people have consecrated to the Supreme Being. Never has the world which He created offered to Him a spectacle so worthy of His notice. He has seen reigning on the earth tyranny, crime, and imposture. He sees at this moment a whole nation, grappling with all the oppressions of the human race.'

THE DEATH OF MARAT

One of the first and most famous executions of a National Convention member came not on the order of the Committee for Public Safety, but at the hand of a Girondin. Jean-Paul Marat was a prominent Montagnard revolutionary who made regular attacks on his Girondin rivals in his newspaper, *L'Ami du Peuple* ('The Friend of the People'). This led to Marat's arrest and trial before the Revolutionary Tribunal, where he was accused of promoting violence and the suspension of the Assembly. Marat disputed the claims and won his case, signalling the ascent of the Montagnards and the decline of the Girondins.

After the trial, Marat was all but housebound by a skin condition for which he took regular, medicinal baths. It was in his bath that Marat had an audience with Girondin member Charlotte Corday, who had brought him a list of so-called traitors. When Marat promised the members would be executed, Corday stabbed him through the chest with a dagger and punctured his heart. Marat died within minutes and Corday was executed by guillotine for the murder.

The Supreme Being was an invention of Robespierre's that supposedly symbolized the divine hand that was guiding the revolution. The festival took place around a manmade mountain on the Champ de Mars. At the top of this mountain, Robespierre appeared before the crowd styled as the Supreme Being. It was a monumental political blunder that confirmed Robespierre as a new emperor in waiting. Behind closed doors, his enemies now called for his head.

Robespierre made his situation worse by a conspicuous three-week absence from the Committee. He had promised to provide a new list exposing more enemies of state, but then failed to come and provide it. Many suspected their name was next on Robespierre's list; their plot against him was an attempt to save their own lives.

When Robespierre next stood to address the Convention, he was shouted down with cries of 'Down with the tyrant! Arrest him!' Dumbfounded, he fell silent. Someone shouted that 'the blood of Danton chokes him'. Robespierre was outlawed as a traitor and arrested, but was freed by loyal guardsmen. Now he was one of the fugitives, hiding in the Hôtel de Ville. With Robespierre were his brother Augustin, and Committee members Philippe-François-Joseph Le Bas, Georges Auguste Couthon and Louis Antoine Léon de Saint-Just. It was suggested they could mount a new coup in the name of the people, but at 2 a.m. their fate banged at the door.

BELOW: Robespierre's Cult of the Supreme Being, created to become the new state religion, was a step too far for his revolutionary colleagues. He would be executed only weeks later.

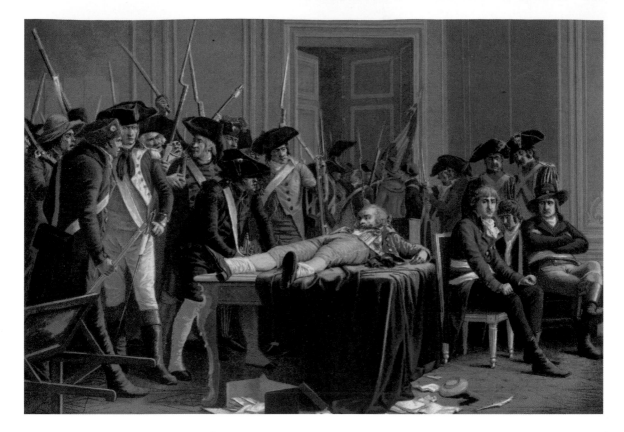

When the arresting guards broke in, Robespierre's supporters panicked. Augustin Robespierre tried to escape by jumping from a window, breaking both of his legs. Le Bas shot himself dead, and Couthon, who was lame, was found at the bottom of the stairwell. Saint-Just simply surrendered. Robespierre himself was shot in the face, shattering his jaw. It is unclear if the bullet came from his own pistol or a soldier's musket. So it was that Robespierre, the great rhetorician who had risen to the top, spent his last hours unable to utter a word. The next day, half dead, Robespierre met his end at the guillotine scaffold. He was said to have ushered a blood-curling scream as the blade came down.

The Terror ended with Robespierre's death, but the executions did not. Instead, the slaughter of those associated with Robespierre and other so-called traitors of the revolution continued under the new White Terror. The numbers killed during the Reign of Terror, however, would remain unsurpassed. Conservative estimates put the nationwide number guillotined at more than 16,500; 2600 of these were in Paris alone. A further 25,000 were killed in summary executions across France. Some say the Terror claimed as many as 55,000 lives in total. Following the Terror, extremism was replaced by moderation as a new government, the Directory, took over from the Convention. By 1800, the revolution was over.

Then, just over two decades after the monarchy had been overthrown, Paris welcomed a new ruler into Paris: the general Napoleon Bonaparte. However, with the crowning of this new king in all but name, France was a different nation. The revolution had shaken off its medieval torpor, thrown down the corrupt rule of its absolute sovereigns, and hurled itself into a new age. Paris, the city at the heart of the new French Empire, began its transformation into the City of Light.

ABOVE: No-one knows for sure who fired the shots into Robespierre's face, but the great orator and terror of the revolution went to his execution half-dead and unable to speak.

EMPIRE AND INSURRECTION

Paris awoke from its revolutionary terror and royalist oppression, but these spectres would constantly return. Between 1800 and 1871, royal restoration, repression and poverty sparked successive revolts. The period would end almost as it began, with an emperor called Napoleon, a foreign invasion and a blood-soaked revolution.

NAPOLEON BONAPARTE WAS believed to be a supporter of the French Revolution, but in 1804 appeared to spurn everything it represented by crowning himself emperor. This, he argued, was a necessary evil, as a dictatorship was the only way to defeat France's foreign enemies and bring order and unity to the fractured republic.

Napoleon's victories on the battlefield were legend: his routing of the Austrians and Russians at Austerlitz and Marengo brought him fame and glory and seemed to justify his imperial role. But his domestic policies repelled veterans of the revolution, above all when he invited exiled nobles to return to France and resurrected Catholicism as the state religion.

In Paris, Napoleon introduced great building works, including new bridges, the widening of the Champs-Élysées, and plans for the Arc de Triomphe. In doing so, Napoleon sold Parisians his vision for a vast, monumental Imperial capital, a place he was determined to make 'the most beautiful city that could exist.' For the people of Paris, this was something of a relief. Their lives since the revolution

OPPOSITE: Revolutionaries stream over the Pont d'Arcole towards the Hôtel de Ville during the 1830 July Revolution. Napoleon had led a similar charge across the bridge in 1796.

had been dominated by political assassinations, poverty, food shortages, and occasional street riots. The memory of the revolution hung over the city like a shroud and Parisians wanted no more violence; the smell of blood lingering in the Place de la Concorde was allegedly so strong that horses refused to cross it. At the simplest level, Napoleon had brought stability, bread and peace to a grateful Parisian population.

But in 1812, everything changed. Napoleon, spurred on by hubris, invaded Russia at the head of a massive 600,000-man army. It was a disaster: Napoleon's own scorched earth policy meant his men had nothing to eat as they made their bitter retreat through a Russian winter. More than half a million lives were lost. Napoleon's failure in Russia would be exacerbated by a decisive battlefield defeat in Leipzig. This time, he retreated into France with the armies of Russia, Prussia and Austria in pursuit.

Paris had received news of Leipzig, but few suspected the city would be subject to a foreign invasion until refugees of the *Grande Armee* began streaming through its gates. A rag-tag procession of deserters, refugees and wounded filled the streets, where they begged, died, and terrified onlookers with news of violent reprisals by Russia. The city quickly reached fever pitch: the hospitals cleared out their insane and elderly to make way for the wounded, as morgues reached capacity and bodies were hoisted into the Seine. Parisians cut down trees to make barricades across streets and shops were boarded up against looting. Then, in late March, a cry went up from the city walls: 'The Cossacks are coming!'

The allied armies bombed the city and then invaded. The battle was short, lasting only a few hours before an armistice was signed and the clatter of the

BELOW: Napoleon leads the bitter retreat from Moscow in 1812. Over 500,000 of Napoleon's 600,000 soldiers were lost during the campaign.

NAPOLEON'S CORONATION

ABOVE: Napoleon rewards himself with the ultimate accolade: the crown of the Emperor of France.

The Duchess of Abrantes was a Parisian socialite and guest at Napoleon's imperial coronation. She was a lover of the writer Honoré de Balzac, who helped her compile her memoirs, which included this extract:

'Napoleon, as he passed along, was greeted by heartfelt expressions of enthusiastic love and attachment. On his arrival at Notre Dame, he ascended the throne, which was erected in front of the grand altar. Josephine took her place beside him, surrounded by the assembled sovereigns of Europe. Napoleon appeared singularly calm… The length of the ceremony, however, seemed to weary him, and I saw him several times check a yawn… During the ceremony of anointing, the Holy Father delivered that impressive prayer… But just as the Pope was about to take the crown, called the crown of Charlemagne, from the altar, Napoleon seized it and placed it on his own head! At that moment he was really handsome, and his countenance was lighted up with an expression of which no words can convey an idea. He had removed the wreath of laurel which he wore on entering the church, and which encircles his brow in the fine picture of Gerard. The crown was, perhaps, in itself, less becoming to him; but the expression excited by the act of putting it on, rendered him perfectly handsome.' (Duchess of Abrantes, *Memoirs*, translated by Gerard Shelley)

THE CATACOMBS

During his reign, Napoleon ordered the city's catacombs to be opened to take the overflow from the Saints-Innocents cemetery. Two million corpses had been buried in the Saints-Innocents over the centuries and in the late eighteenth century the cemetery had literally burst its banks with bodies. Rotting heads and severed corpses from the recent Terror rose to the surface, while the sheer weight of longer-buried bodies had broken through the basements of several nearby houses. The fetid air was reportedly so strong that several people died from the fumes. The cemetery's corpses were exhumed and transported to the catacombs and smaller cemeteries on the city's outskirts, including the Père Lachaise. For many years, these areas became the dark provinces of gravediggers and priests, who carried out their night-time work of prayer and corpse removal by lamplight.

LEFT: The catacombs today are estimated to house the remains of between six and seven million dead Parisians.

dreaded Cossack hooves was heard on the Champs-Élysées. However, there was no punishment for the wrongs committed by Napoleon against Russia. Tsar Alexander I promised that no reprisals would be imposed and that Paris was now under his 'special protection'. Instead of rebelling against their new occupiers, Paris began to celebrate. The occupiers, in return, behaved themselves. The Cossacks were mostly restrained in their vices and became a familiar sight at Paris restaurants. Here, nervous about being caught drinking by their superiors, Cossacks dined fast and without fuss – giving birth to the Parisian 'bistro', after the Russian for 'quickly'. Then, almost as fast as they appeared, the occupying armies were gone. In their place was a new ruler: King Louis XVIII, brother of the recently beheaded Louis XVI. The monarchy was back.

The Restoration

If there was a collective groan at the sight of the Bourbon king Louis XVIII, a pompous and obese figure, Paris was hardly more enthusiastic about Napoleon's return to the capital after 11 months of exile on Elba. Louis XVIII fled to England, but Napoleon's grip on power lasted for a mere 100 days. In the end, Napoleon's army was famously defeated on the battlefield of Waterloo and he was banished permanently to the rocky outcrop of Saint Helena in the Atlantic Ocean. A succession of monarchs followed, including the reinstated Louis XVIII, his son Charles X, and finally Louis Philippe, the last king of France.

Paris during these changes was a city profoundly divided and ill at ease. There were a multitude of contending factions, including Jacobins, monarchists, Catholics and Bonapartists, and each seemed only one grievance away from becoming a rioting mob. The ideals of the Revolution seemed a distant memory as the city's nobles and wealthy bourgeoisie cohabitated uneasily with the dirt-poor masses. The group that had suffered most from revolution and its squalid aftermath was the working class.

Before the restoration, Paris was a hellish place. Gambling houses and brothels surrounded the Palais-Royal; the city centre was a hive of violence and vice. Beggars mugged the rich in dark alleyways. There were a reported 1000 beggars in Paris at that time, many of them former soldiers who had deserted or become unemployed after Napoleon's exile. These became the hard core of the Paris underclass; their brutality towards unsuspecting Parisians became the stuff of urban nightmares, with rapes, beatings and murder commonplace.

'People, animals, excrement and rotting garbage were crammed together.'

Working-class areas such as Saint-Marceau, nicknamed 'suburb suffering', became even more violent and desperate under the restoration. People, animals, excrement and rotting garbage were crammed together. A filthy haze was said to cover many such areas; officials decreed that pregnant women had to be moved to more hygienic surroundings. These women soon filled the hospitals, alongside sick vagrant children, and the insane. Venereal disease was rife and the Hôpital du Midi was set up to treat its victims. The waiting list, however, was impossibly long, and the city's 75,000 prostitutes ensured that it kept getting longer.

The worst suburbs became no-go areas; public sanitation disappeared. Paris was a disgracefully dirty city under the restoration, but working-class areas

BELOW: Here, the Cossack invaders of Paris make camp before riding into the city. Tsar Alexander ordered there be no reprisals for Napoleon's attack on Russia.

DESCRIPTIONS OF POVERTY

Nineteenth-century writer Victor Hugo described the
Parisian slums in his novels, and was in turn criticized
for adding to the terror felt by the middle class:

'A street, at that time, without houses, unpaved,
bordered with scrubby trees, grass-grown or muddy,
according to the season, and running squarely up to
the wall encircling Paris… As far as the eye could
reach there was nothing to be seen but the public
shambles, the city wall, and here and there the side
of the factory, resembling a barrack or a monastery;
on all sides, miserable hovels and heaps of rubbish,
old walls as black as widow's weeds, and new
walls as white as winding-sheets; on all sides,
parallel rows of trees, buildings in straight lines,
flat structures, long, cold perspectives, and the
gloomy sameness of right angles.' (Victor Hugo,
Les Misérables, translated by Charles Wilbour)

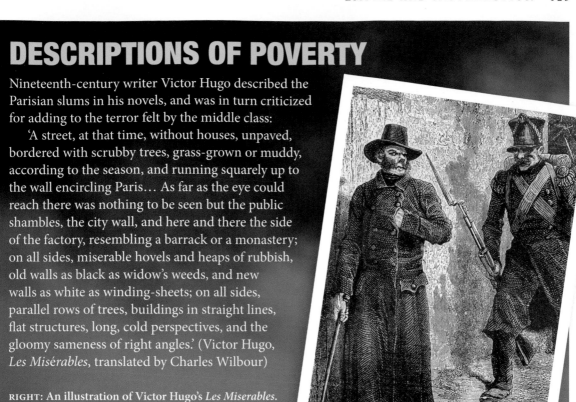

RIGHT: An illustration of Victor Hugo's *Les Miserables*.
Here, Inspector Javert is shown hunting for Valjean,
the novel's main protagonist.

were often simply left to rot. There was no rubbish collection, so the waste from
Paris' 250,000 households was simply left in the street. Raw sewage ran into the
Seine, the river used for washing and drinking, and collected in stinking deposits
on its banks. Run-off from an abattoir built on the site of the former Gibbet of
Montfaucon further contaminated the water supply. In 1832, the city fell prey to
the worst cholera epidemic in its history.

The first cholera sufferers began appearing at the Hôtel-Dieu hospital in
March, displaying a wide range of symptoms that baffled the doctors: fever, chest
pains, vomiting, headaches, apoplexy. They had come from the working-class
suburbs at the city limits – the 12th, 9th and 7th arrondissements – but soon cases
from all over the city were being admitted. The hospital was quickly overrun; by
the end of the month every admission was for cholera and none were discharged.

During April, carts piled with corpses clattered through the streets and a
dense odour of death lingered over the city. One of the most perplexing aspects of
the cholera outbreak was that the symptoms could manifest themselves gradually,
or otherwise come on without warning. Some died within hours of discovering
symptoms, while others languished for days and were said to resemble the dead
even while they were still alive, their tongues becoming ice-cold. Little was known
about the disease or how to deal with it. A Paris official recommended that to
prevent catching the disease, people should take hot baths infused with vinegar,
salt and mustard, and consume lime tea.

OPPOSITE: A collective
groan went up at the
coronation of Louis XVIII,
brother to the recently
beheaded Louis XVI. The
monarchy was back.

CHOLERA CATCHING

German poet Heinrich Heine was in Paris at the time of the cholera outbreak, which he described in his journals.

'That night, the balls were more crowded than usual; hilarious laughter all but drowned the roar of music; people grew hot in the chahut, a fairly unequivocal dance, and gulped all kinds of ices and other cold drinks – when suddenly the merriest of the harlequins felt a chill in his legs, took off his mask, and to the amazement of all revealed a violet-blue face. It was soon discovered that this was no joke; the laughter died, and several wagon loads were driven directly from the ball to the Hôtel-Dieu, the main hospital, where they arrived in their gaudy fancy dress and promptly died, too… those dead were said to have been buried so fast that not even their checkered fool's clothes were taken off them; and merrily as they lived they now lie in their graves…

"We shall all be stuck into the sack, one after another," said my servant with a sigh every morning, when he announced how many had died or the loss of someone known. The expression "stuck into the sack" was no mere figure of speech, for coffins were soon wanting, and the greater part of the dead were buried in bags… those watchers of the dead, who with a grim indifference counted out the sacks to the men who buried them; and how the latter, as they piled them on their carts, repeated the number in lower tones, or complained harshly that they had received one corpse too few, over which there often arose a strange dispute. And I remember how two small boys with sorrowful faces stood by, and that one asked if I could tell him which sack his father was in.' (Heinrich Heine, *The Works of Heinrich Heine*, translated by Charles Leland)

By the end of the six-month epidemic, nearly 19,000 had died. Most of the victims were from the working-class suburbs, although the disease afflicted rich as well as poor. Many accused King Louis Philippe of poisoning the water used by working-class areas; the link between poor sanitation, overcrowding, and contaminated water systems was not discovered until 1854.

The July Revolution

Cholera preceded insurrection, a recurrent visitor to nineteenth-century Paris. Revolt was the people's response to the unpopular rule of Charles X, who had succeeded Louis XVIII in 1824 and seemed bent on returning the monarchy to its pre-revolutionary pomp. In his short tenure, Charles sought to become an absolute monarch: he reasserted the power of the Catholic Church, compensated aristocrats dispossessed by the revolution, and restricted the growing power of the press. He tried to curry public favour by invading Algeria in 1830, but this drained the royal coffers and had the opposite effect.

By 1830, the French economy had slowed to a halt, unemployment was high, and an agricultural crisis led to food shortages in Paris. However, the tipping point came only when Charles announced he would suspend the constitution and reform the electoral system. The next day, a crowd gathered in the sweltering heat outside the Palais-Royal, shouting 'Down with the Bourbons!' and smashing some of the 2000 streetlights that had been recently installed. The next morning, soldiers closed down the city's newspapers, further inflaming the Palais-Royal crowd. Stones were hurled at the soldiers, who responded by firing into the crowd. The violence spilled into the evening as the protest turned into a riot. What followed was three days of running battles around rue Saint-Antoine and the Place de Gréve known as *les Trois Glorieuses*.

In response, Charles X commanded the unpopular General Auguste de Marmont to repress the rioters, who had established city-wide barricades and were hurling paving stones, roof tiles and flowerpots at the soldiers. Marmont's plan was to guard important buildings such as the Palais-Royal, the Palais de Justice and Hôtel de Ville, while also cutting off the city's thoroughfares, including its bridges. The plan was doomed to fail: Marmont simply did not have enough troops to guard the buildings as well as suppress the rebellion.

Many of Marmont's soldiers openly deserted, while others joined the rioters. Marmont sent a note to Charles X: 'Sire, it is no longer a riot, it is a revolution. It is urgent for Your Majesty to take measures for pacification. The honour of the crown can still be saved. Tomorrow, perhaps, there will be no more time…. I await with impatience Your Majesty's orders.' Charles, however, with a number of his supporters, had holed up at Versailles, where he procrastinated.

By day three of *les Trois Glorieuses*, the revolutionaries had thrown up 4000 barricades around the streets of Paris and flew tricolour flags from the rooftops. Marmont froze with indecision: he did not order up new reserves, nor try to arrest the main leaders of the revolt; instead he helplessly awaited orders from the king, which were not forthcoming.

By the afternoon, the revolutionaries had sacked the Louvre and Tuileries palaces and had grown drunk from the vast royal wine cellars. The other

BELOW: The 1832 outbreak begins. It would become the worst cholera epidemic in the history of Paris.

OPPOSITE: Charles X is pictured entering Paris with all the pomp and pageantry of the absolute sovereign he wished to be. The penultimate king of the restored monarchy, Charles' rule led to the July Revolution.

BELOW: In Eugene Delacroix's *Liberty Leading the People*, Parisians from all walks of life rise up for the July Revolution's *les Trois Glorieuses*.

ABOVE: Known as the 'Citizen King', Louis Philippe liked giving the impression that he was a friend of the people, but he kept a spare pair of gloves for working-class handshakes.

buildings that Marmont wanted to guard also fell. Interestingly, the drunken mob took care not to be destructive, making great pains to protect the city's precious artworks and cultural artefacts. By the afternoon of 29 July, Paris was theirs.

The uprising now over, Charles X and his son renounced their rights to the throne and departed for exile in Britain. In Charles' place, Louis Philippe from the house of Orleans was crowned, but only as a constitutional monarch. The July Revolution, the first to be truly won and fought by the city's working classes, was hailed for finishing the job started in 1789. A brave new world was now awaited; it did not arrive.

Louis Philippe was quick to distance himself from Charles' conservative rule, cultivating an image of himself as a bourgeois businessman who would dispense with all vestiges of absolutism. He liked to be seen as a champion of the people who called his workmen 'my friends'. He would, however, also carry two pairs of gloves: one to shake hands with the working classes and another for merchants, businessmen and aristocrats.

The working class felt sold out by the bourgeois politicians who had crowned Louis Philippe after the July Revolution. The atmosphere on the streets was volatile and uneasy, and violence was never far away. Hundreds had been killed during riots in 1831, and in 1834, following the cholera outbreak, another round began. In 1835, a Corsican immigrant tried to assassinate Louis Philippe. For this, he won the dubious honour of being the first would-be regicide to be spared torture before his execution.

Louis Philippe's problem was that he wished to create a comfortable world where the upwardly mobile bourgeoisie could thrive. As in other centres of Western Europe at this time, Paris was enjoying many of the middle-class fruits of the industrial revolution. Described by Balzac as 'The leader of civilization, the most adorable of fatherlands', Paris boasted covered shopping arcades and the first grand department store; beautiful railway stations and an integrated public transport system; a burgeoning art trade; great scientific centres of learning; plays, concerts, theatre; and, of course, restaurants and world-class dining. It was the capital of the *flaneur*, a hedonistic man of leisure, strolling idly through the City of Light and drinking in the crowd and the creative energy of the age. A *flaneur*, according to the great poet Charles Baudelaire, was the artist-poet of the modern metropolis. Balzac described *flanerie* as 'the gastronomy of the eye'.

The constant flood of novels and newspapers in Paris was a European-wide phenomenon made possible by the 1843 invention of the rotary printing press. Parisians loved this influx of print partly because they loved reading about themselves: the city supported 26 different newspapers at this time. Print also cast a shadow: potboilers by writers such as Balzac and Eugène Sue terrified the bourgeoisie with tales about the city's seething underclass. Some newspapers called on the working classes to rise up in rebellion against repression.

The most famous exemplar of the new socialism in Europe was the Cologne newspaper of Karl Marx, the *New Rhenish Newspaper: Organ of Democracy*. Marx, whose *Communist Manifesto*, co-written with Friedrich Engels, was electrifying the continent, cited Paris as the revolutionary heartland of Europe. He called on the city's workers to revolt once more. In 1848, the workers of Paris answered the call and became part of a revolutionary wave that swept through Europe. The revolutions of 1848, however, would end in failure for the socialist movement; by the end of the year a dictator had been installed in every European country.

> **'Potboilers terrified the bourgeoisie with tales about the city's seething underclass.'**

The 1848 Revolution

Paris was in crisis before the 1848 Revolution. The population had reached one million, but the city did not have the infrastructure to support it. Over a third of working-class Parisians crammed themselves into overcrowded five-storey dwellings in famously dangerous suburbs, such as Saint-Victor and Saint-Marcel. The Île de la Cité was, as ever, a sinister labyrinth of dark alleys, brothels and urban brigandry.

BELOW: This 1832 image shows Louis Philippe putting his hand over the mouth of a female printer in 'the workshop of the freedom of the press'.

The poor faced overcrowding, hunger and unemployment. Harvest failures in 1846 and 1847 had led to famine; a third of the city's adult population was unemployed. Writers such as Louis Blanc called for 'the right to work', but Louis Philippe resisted reform or help for the masses. The tinder awaited a flame.

'Paris erupted in war: omnibuses used as barricades, trees were felled to build others.'

The last straw was a decree in February 1848 outlawing banquets by political activists to raise funds. A crowd of working-class and bourgeois Parisians gathered outside the Ministry of Foreign Affairs. Another crowd began building barricades. A running battle soon started between the protesters and the king's soldiers. The following day, one soldier nervously discharged his musket into the crowd at the Ministry of Foreign Affairs, and the other soldiers followed his lead. Fifty-two people died in the ensuing massacre.

Paris erupted in war: omnibuses were thrown over and used as barricades, trees were felled to build others. Louis Philippe abdicated and fled to England. France's 1000-year-old monarchy was at an end – again. Hours after Louis Philippe had left, a crowd stormed and ransacked the Tuileries and the Palais Royal. Furniture and paintings of the monarchs were thrown through windows, and the royal throne was carried through the city and set alight in the Place de la Bastille. The Second Republic of France had begun.

BELOW: Royal carriages are set alight during the 1848 Revolution. The Second Republic of France followed.

The Republic proclaimed the freedom of the press, freedom of assembly, universal male suffrage, and a 10-hour working day. Progressive policies aside, the Parisian poor were still going hungry and after a few months little in their lives had changed. The numbers of unemployed had reached over 180,000. Many felt

The conqueror of Algeria, General Louis-Eugène Cavaignac was brought in to crush the Parisian rebellion. He became known as 'the butcher of June.'

BALZAC

Honoré de Balzac wrote more than 90 novels and captured many of the preoccupations and prejudices of Paris' inhabitants. Like many of the authors of his time, Balzac was horrified by Paris' underbelly and complained that the city had 'more foreigners and provincials than Parisians'. Himself born in the provinces, Balzac's dislike of foreigners summed up a general mood of nineteenth-century Parisian xenophobia, especially against the English and Algerians. Balzac, however, thought the working classes were little better than the 'savages' being discovered on the newly colonized continent of Africa. His descriptions of the city's natives both terrified and titillated his readers:

'One of those sights in which most horror is to be encountered is, surely, the general aspect of the Parisian populace – a people fearful to behold, gaunt, yellow, tawny… men whose twisted and contorted faces give out at every pore the instinct, the desire, the poisons with which their brains are pregnant; not faces so much as masks; masks of weakness, masks

ABOVE: When not writing, Balzac was known as a socially ostentatious dandy who seemed aware of his own genius.

of strength, masks of misery, masks of joy, masks of hypocrisy.' (Honoré de Balzac, *The Girl With the Golden Eyes*, translated by Ellen Marriage)

they had been sold out by the bourgeoisie, who were now pulling the strings of the republican government. In June, the Parisian working class came out once again in revolt; this time they were not joined by the middle classes. On 23 June, barricades were hastily thrown up as rioting and street fighting began. Now, however, government troops were going to come down hard on the insurrectionists.

General Louis-Eugène Cavaignac, fresh from conquering Algeria for France, was in charge of crushing the 'Red' rebellion. He brought 30,000 of his army regulars and aimed heavy artillery at the barricades. The rebels had little chance; within three days of fighting more than 1500 were killed. Corpses were piled high on the rue Blanche, and others rotted where they fell. More than 10,000 rebels were arrested and either shipped to Algeria or thrown en masse into prison dungeons.

Although the republic lived on in name, it was clear the army was now the true master of France. In December, presidential elections were won by Louis Napoleon III, nephew of Bonaparte. Napoleon insisted he was 'above politics', and promised a return to the heady days of his uncle. In 1852, after failing to amend the constitution to give him longer in office, Napoleon staged a coup and crowned himself emperor. The Second Empire of France now began.

The Second Empire

Napoleon was variously described as a short, thickset man with dull eyes, who was cold, boorish and unsure of himself, but also charming, romantic and intelligent. The statesman Adolphe Thiers, who had brought Napoleon Bonaparte's ashes home from Saint Helena in 1840, famously described his nephew as 'a cretin'.

Napoleon, however, was a man with large notions of himself and high aspirations for Paris. Declaring that he would be another Augustus, because 'Augustus made Rome a city of marble', Napoleon transformed Paris into the modern city we know today. In charge of the reconstruction was Georges-Eugène Haussmann, who brought to Paris its great boulevards: 'We ripped open the belly of old Paris, the neighbourhood of revolt and barricades, and cut a large opening through the almost impenetrable maze of alleys, piece by piece.'

Haussmann's plan was to open Paris up, clear away the alleys and slum housing and encourage the free movement of the bourgeoisie and, therefore capital, around the city. The boulevards would enable troops to quickly access any part of the city and were built deliberately wide so barricades could not be built across them.

The effect was to turn Paris into a light, prosperous city, illuminated by 30,000 gas lamps. This was a cityscape of boulevards, apartment blocks and black, wrought-

BELOW: This 1858 map of Paris details in red the boulevards built by Napoleon III and Haussmann during the Second Empire.

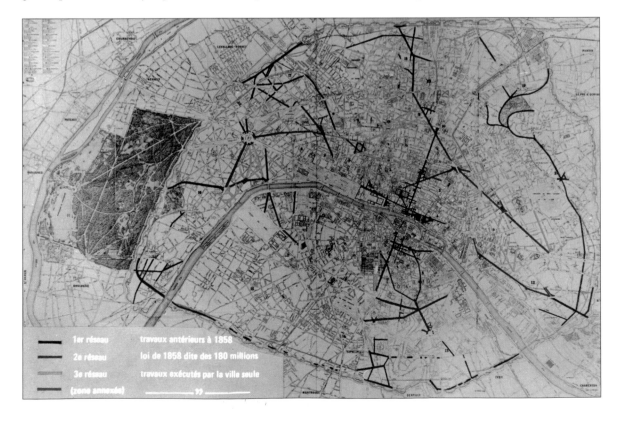

	1er réseau	travaux antérieurs à 1858
	2e réseau	loi de 1858 dite des 180 millions
	3e réseau	travaux exécutés par la ville seule
	(zone annexée)	99

iron railings. With the city's underclass pushed into more distant suburbs, the rich central Parisians were free to follow the social and moral tone laid down by their emperor. Napoleon sought to revive the carnival atmosphere last seen in Paris under Louis XIV. Hunts returned to the woods of Fontainebleau, lace and feathered hats came back into fashion, and extravagant masked balls were held in lavish halls.

Often these balls were highly sexualized affairs, featuring scantily clad models and orgies in the antechambers off the main ballroom. In the time-honoured Parisian tradition, the carnal appetites of the upper classes were reflected below – around 30,000 prostitutes were said to be working the city at that time, with some willing to accept a night at the theatre or a restaurant dinner in lieu of payment. Cabaret was another form of theatre that became popular, although the erotic nature of its most famous dance, the cancan, was derided by some for its coarse Algerian roots.

While many enjoyed the growing prosperity of Napoleon's Paris, the working classes were once again left wondering where it had all gone wrong. The Revolutions of 1789, 1830 and 1848 had promised a new, egalitarian beginning for French society, but at the end of every uprising only the bourgeoisie had seemed to profit. Now, in the new Paris, the working classes had been pushed to the city limits where the ghettos created by Haussmann formed the dark shadow of the prosperous centre. Beneath the surface of Parisian society was a seething bitterness.

The Siege of Paris

BELOW: A lithograph showing the glass oval building of the 1867 International Exposition.

The zenith of Napoleon's reign was the 1867 International Exposition, where visitors could take balloon rides over the large, oval glass building showcasing the industrial accomplishments of modern society. Within a few years, however, Napoleon's glittering new Paris would be lying in flames.

Napoleon's nemesis was Otto von Bismarck, the conniving Prussian chancellor who wanted to chance his duelling arm against his neighbouring rival. After an exchange of sabre rattling, Napoleon simply fell into the elephant trap set by Bismarck; on 16 July 1870, he declared war on Prussia.

By 1 September, Napoleon's reign was over. He surrendered to King Wilhelm I of Prussia after losing the Battle of Sedan, and left Paris to fend for itself as the enemy army approached. The reaction to Napoleon's capitulation was at first disgust and then anger, followed by delight: the empire was over! A mob stormed the Tuileries palace, smashing busts of the emperor and eradicating any vestiges of imperial rule. As a Third Republic was declared, it was assumed that Bismarck would halt his march on Paris, but he did not. On 15 September, the Germans were at the city gates.

A four-month siege of Paris began a few days later. Inside, 400,000 troops who had retreated from the front started strengthening the 34km-long (21 mile) wall built around the city in 1840 by the statesman Adolphe Thiers. It was this that allowed the Parisians to resist the invaders.

Bismarck and King Wilhelm made their headquarters at Versailles, where, in the palace's hall of mirrors, Wilhelm famously declared himself Emperor of Germany. In Paris, those behind the walls had stocked up the city's supplies, including more than 200,000 sheep. This would not, however, be enough to keep the besieged population fed. By October, trees were felled along the Champs-Élysées for firewood and Parisians were dining on horsemeat.

ABOVE: The 1870 Battle of Villiers was one of the attempted French breakouts during the Siege of Paris. Over 9000 French soldiers died in the battle.

SIEGE MENU, 1870

These were some of the dishes served in high-end Paris restaurants in late 1870, including *Café Voisin*, which served haunch of wolf with venison sauce as its main on Christmas Day.

Consommé of elephant
Grilled dog's liver
Minced saddle of cat with mayonnaise
Filleted shoulder of dog with peas
Stuffed donkey's head
Rat ragout in brown mustard sauce
Bear chops with pepper sauce

Roasted camel English style
Antelope terrine with truffles
Braised kangaroo
Dog gigot flanked by baby rats
Begonia in juice
Plum pudding in juice with horse marrow

Several military breakouts had been tried to connect the Paris army with French troops left in the provinces, but all failed. A more inventive method of escape involved the city's hot air balloons. Put into regular service, the balloons dispatched more than two million letters during the siege, as well as several hundred passengers. The cost of a balloon letter was 20 centimes, compared with 50 centimes per word for letters sent by carrier pigeon. To post mail in this way a letter was written out on a large piece of cardboard, photographed, and a 40 by 55mm (1½ by 2in) print folded and dispatched.

Letters by pigeon carrier did not have the same success rate as the balloon post, however, especially when the Prussian army employed falcons to intercept the carriers.

Parisian inventiveness did not end with hot air balloons. It was suggested that Paris' prostitutes be armed with pins dipped in poison, which, if the city should fall, could be used on the Prussian soldiers during their most vulnerable moments. Arms, too, were being made from every available material: church bells were melted down to make cannon; bronze and tin were used for musket cartridges. The cannons would be a pivotal factor in the violence that followed the Prussian siege, which by December was taking a heavy toll on the city.

It had become clear that the Prussians intended to starve Paris out, and the tactic was having an effect. Dogs and cats were now on the menu, as the city had run out of horses. Paris' fondness for culinary decoration persisted despite the siege; fattened cats were laid out in the centre of a dish and surrounded by mice in the form of small sausages. According to the writer Théophile Gautier, household pets became aware of their owner 'regarding them in a strange manner, and that under the pretext of caressing them, his hand was feeling like a fingers of a butcher, to ascertain the state of their embonpoint.'

The consumption of rats also became something of a delicacy, with special sauces developed to hide the shape of the meat. It was the general consensus that the brewery rat was superior to the sewer rat, although good rat pie could disguise the taste of either. Class once again determined who was fed and who went

> ‘The consumption of rats also became something of a delicacy.’

hungry. The upper classes dined out on fresh meat being supplied to restaurants by the city zoo. Camel, wolf, antelope and the zoo's elephants Castor and Pollux were on the menu, while its carnivores were considered too dangerous to approach and left to starve. At the other end of the social spectrum, the working classes were forced into the medieval practice of digging up corpses and boiling their bones as stock.

To add to Paris' misery, Bismarck began a relentless shelling of the city with his large-calibre Krupp cannon, which had dazzled the crowds at the 1867 Paris Exposition a few years earlier. Bismarck's strategy was to terrorize the civilian population so they would force their commanders to surrender. It did not work: Parisians instead became more determined than ever. The city's middle class, however, was becoming nervous. The shells raining down on the city were destroying their businesses and assets and their ability to make money. In February, they forced the National Assembly to broker a peace deal with the Prussians. But the city's poor had suffered the most from the siege, and, unlike the bourgeoisie, their shattered lives would not be as easy to restart. They would not be sold out again. So, in spring 1871, their new revolution began.

The Paris Commune

The terms of the armistice between the Prussians and Adolphe Thiers, now president of the new Republican Assembly, included disarming the national French army. However, when the army came to round up the 200 cannons left at

BELOW: Prussian soldiers man their heavy artillery during the Siege of Paris. The Prussian aim was to drive ordinary Parisians crazy with fear. It didn't work.

LAWS OF EXECUTION

When news reached the Commune that the Assembly was shooting prisoners, it ordered an immediate retaliation. It issued the Decree on Hostages, which made it law to imprison anyone accused of complicity with the Versailles Government after a short trial before a jury. Three hostages would then be executed for every Communard prisoner shot by the Assembly. In response, the Assembly passed its own law giving military tribunals the power to execute all prisoners within 24 hours of arrest. The novelist Émile Zola wrote of the events in the newspaper *La Cloche*:

'Thus we citizens of Paris are placed between two terrible laws; the law of suspects brought back by the Commune and the law on rapid executions which will certainly be approved by the Assembly. They are not fighting with cannon shots, they are slaughtering each other with decrees.'

Paris' Montmartre, the people protested. They were not prepared to surrender the city's guns to a new bourgeois Republican government that had made Versailles and not Paris the seat of power. The crowd became an angry mob and shot dead two army generals, whose bodies they strung up.

The army evacuated the city and a group of 64 representatives gathered on the steps of the Hôtel de Ville, raised a red flag, and declared that Paris was now in the hands of the Commune. The group was an odd assortment that included National Guard Members, Jacobins, anarchists, revolutionary feminists, and various immigrants, including the Polish activist Jaroslaw Dombrowski. The Commune proclaimed itself to be the true revolution of the people. Members of the Commune immediately began writing out new laws for workers, such as prohibiting night shifts for bakers.

However, in delaying an immediate march on Versailles to take control of the Republican Assembly, the Commune lost its valuable initiative. By the time the Commune's National Guard marched towards Versailles, the regular army of the Republican Assembly had had time to regroup and was prepared for the assault. When this came, as the greying dawn turned to daylight, the 27,000-strong Communard army was utterly overwhelmed by Assembly artillery fire. The Communards who fled back to Paris assumed the army would be unwilling to shoot any left behind. They were wrong: the army was told that this was now a civil war and prisoners were to be executed, not captured.

Now it was the turn of the Assembly to march on Paris while, behind the city walls, Parisians enjoyed something of a festival atmosphere. On the night of 21 May, a concert performed by more than 1000 musicians was held at the Tuileries Palace. At the end of the concert, an officer of the National Guard announced that Adolphe Thiers had promised to enter Paris the day before, and as he had not, all attending were invited back for another concert the following Sunday.

Only hours after this announcement, a stream of 70,000 soldiers picked their way through gaps in the city's western defences. The soldiers were welcomed by the middle-class inhabitants of the suburb of Saint-Cloud before marching towards the centre. The Communards hastily threw up barricades to block their way.

OPPOSITE: Representatives of the Commune congregate outside the Hôtel de Ville. Within weeks, the building would be ablaze.

It was a desperate battle: the Communards understood that no quarter would be given, so it was a fight to the death. The bravest held their positions behind the large barricades in the Rue Royale and the Place de la Concorde, but before long, the army had taken the city's key positions. The Communards began a scorched earth policy as they pulled back into increasingly isolated pockets of resistance. Rumours began to circulate of Communard women, *pétroleuses*, throwing incendiary devices into building basements. Now as the Assembly troops pushed forwards, thick columns of black smoke billowed across the sky: Paris was burning.

NEWSPAPER REPORTS

The Times of London issued a daily report on the suppression of the Paris Commune, which consisted of a few paragraphs of descriptive prose filed by Paris correspondents via telegraph. The below extracts have been compiled from the reports from 25–29 May:

BELOW: The violent put-down of the Commune would result in the destruction of large sections of Paris.

'New fires are bursting out in Paris. The insurgents put boxes of petroleum everywhere. Blood runs in the gutters of the streets. The walls of the Tuileries have fallen. The Rue Rivoli is burning. The Versaillists, since Tuesday, are killing all prisoners. I saw numbers of the Communist sympathizers killed, and among them was a young man, handsomely dressed, with hands tied and brains blown out…. Executions of insurgents are constant. The destruction of property is terrible. One-fourth of Paris is estimated to have been destroyed. A dispatch from St. Denis, Friday night, says there are still terrible conflagrations in Paris, the flames of which rise to a great height and illuminate the country for miles around. All human aid seems valueless… The Commune is dying hard. The insurgents fought with desperation in the cemetery of Père-La-Chaise. The insurgents yesterday shot the Archbishop of Paris, the Abbé Duguerry, and 62 other hostages remaining in their possession. The remaining insurgents must now die or surrender. There are rumours of awful cruelties perpetrated by the Versaillists, who are reported to have shot men, women and children found with arms in their hands.' (*The Times*)

By 25 May, a large number of the city's most famous buildings were ablaze: the Tuileries, the Palais-Royal, the Palais de Justice, the Hôtel de Ville. The Assembly soldiers were now executing anyone not in regular army uniform; heavy artillery and the devastating new weapon, the machine gun, were used in the massacre. Those not killed in the fighting were lined up and shot; a priest reported witnessing a group of women being tied together and killed in this way.

The Communards made a last stand at the Père Lachaise Cemetery, where, among the graves of famous Parisians such as Balzac and Delavigne, they were cut down by the dozen. Those left alive were lined up and shot against a wall of the cemetery, known today as the Communards' Wall. Execution by firing squad reached industrial proportions during 'Bloody Week', the days following the end of the revolution; between 15,000 and 25,000 were executed.

The Belle Époque, or 'Beautiful Era', followed the atrocities of the Paris Commune. There seemed an urgent need to wash away the horror that had been committed during the Bloody Week of May 1871, but it could not easily be forgotten. The Commune, which had promised so much in the name of the working classes, had fallen after a brief 72 days. For those on the left, it was a savage lesson about the dangers of resisting the state. Despite every revolution fought out in Paris between 1789 and 1871, one point had been made undeniably clear: it was the state and not the people that held the reins of power in France.

ABOVE: Once won back, the Communard barricades made handy bunkers for army artillery. This example was photographed on Rue Voltaire.

THE CITY OF LIGHT AND DARK

The Belle Époque was a giddy, optimistic era that contrived to banish the bleak memory of the Commune and re-imagine Paris in a blur of dreamy colours. But, as cultural and industrial innovation swept the city, nothing could disguise its internal divisions. Nor could anyone foresee the catastrophic conflict that would follow.

THE BELLE ÉPOQUE retains its place in the world's memory because the period was recorded by some of the most renowned artists in history. The great Impressionist artists painted a beautiful picture of Paris and France and sold it to the world. It was an era, however, built on the ashes of the Commune.

Many creative figures, including Hugo, Zola, Flaubert, Monet, Cézanne and Renoir, had fled Paris during the worst of the violence, but slowly returned to their broken city. Their initial impressions record a range of emotions. The actress Sarah Bernhardt cursed the 'wretched Commune' and the 'abominable and shameful peace', reporting that everything she touched had a dark, greasy residue and that a 'bitter odour of smoke' lingered everywhere.

Novelist Émile Zola had stayed in Paris writing as cannons boomed and shells whistled over his apartment building; he fled the city when the buildings around him started burning. When he returned he was surprised to find that nothing in his apartment had changed – even the houseplants were still alive. This caused him to ponder whether the whole event had been 'a nasty farce invented to

OPPOSITE: French Marshals Foch and Joffre celebrate victory on the Champs-Élysées in 1919. World War I had left Paris relatively unscathed compared to the destruction of the 1871 Commune.

frighten the children.' Writer Gustave Flaubert, on the other hand, observed the extreme tensions that remained among post-Commune Parisians: 'One half of the population of Paris wants to strangle the other half, and the other half has the same idea; you can read it in the eyes of people passing by.'

Artist Édouard Manet commented that 'Each one lays the blame on his neighbour, but we are all to blame for what has happened.' He also reported in an October 1871 letter to artist Berthe Morisot that Paris was coming back to life: 'I hope, mademoiselle, that you will not stay a long time in Cherbourg. Everybody is returning to Paris; besides, it's impossible to live anywhere else.'

Paris was rebuilt as swiftly as possible: Haussmann's wide boulevards were completed; a new façade was attached to the ruined Hôtel de Ville, based on its Renaissance period design; and the much maligned avant-garde basilica of Sacré-Cœur was built on the butte of Montmartre. For the working class, Sacré-Cœur – dedicated to reconciliation after the fall of the Commune – represented the triumph of the middle class over the city's poor. This was the paradox of Paris after the Commune: a city struggling to find its identity by restyling itself as the City of Light and prosperity. But it kept one muddy foot in the past while dreaming of a splendid future. The Impressionists painted this romantic, chimerical vision in a magnificent blaze of colour; political reality had a different, darker hue.

BELOW: Renoir's *Pont Neuf*, 1872. The artist's new, impressionistic style was considered so radical that he was accused of being a Prussian spy.

CONFUSED IMPRESSIONS

Today the Impressionists' artworks are instantly recognizable for their colourful depictions of everyday Parisian life, but they were widely criticized on their first showing. By abandoning the principles of realism for on-the-spot studies of light and colour, Impressionist artworks were often considered sketches rather than finished pieces; the Académie de Paris rejected the new style outright. Subject matter also presented a problem, with the dreamy scenes of middle-class life seen as a rejection of the plight of the poor. Marxist critic T.J. Clark wondered if Impressionism was 'the house style of the bourgeoisie'.

Pierre-Auguste Renoir had suffered politically for his art before. In 1871, Renoir had been painting along the Seine when he was confronted by a group of Communards observing his work. The Communards could not believe Renoir's picture could be art, and concluded he must be a Prussian spy creating a visual plan of the city. They arrested the artist and took him to be shot. However, at the last moment Renoir was saved by Communard police chief Raoul Rigault, who had once hidden with the artist from the police force of the Second Empire. Rigault embraced Renoir, set him free, and immediately issued him with a pass to leave Paris.

Politics of the Époque

Politics in Paris followed the rapid pace of change affecting all of Europe in the late nineteenth century. After the downfall of the socialist Commune, the Parisian monarchists gained popularity; by the late 1870s it even looked as though a royal restoration was imminent. Then the left made a revival: the Republican government moved its Parlement from Versailles to Paris and freed the first of the Communard prisoners. In 1885, the left was out in force again, when the city mourned the passing of its hero Victor Hugo. In his honour, Paris got drunk and prostitutes reportedly worked for free on the lawns of the Champs-Élysées.

'Everybody is returning to Paris; besides, it's impossible to live anywhere else.'

But only two years later there was a lurch towards belligerent nationalism; General Georges Boulanger was elected to the National Assembly and immediately called for the destruction of Prussia. Alarmed at Boulanger's sabre rattling, assembly statesman Georges Clemenceau deported the general's mistress to Belgium. Although protesters called on Boulanger to march on the Élysée Palace in response, he instead followed his mistress. One year later he committed suicide on her grave.

A far more sinister outbreak of right-wing extremism was the Dreyfus Affair of 1894, a worldwide scandal that exposed a dark flood of Parisian anti-Semitism. Alfred Dreyfus was a Jewish officer of the French army falsely accused of selling military secrets to the Germans. The evidence against Dreyfus was a letter, detailing the technical specifications of a new French cannon, which had been fished from a wastepaper basket and that accusers said was in Dreyfus' handwriting. Despite any proof of his guilt, Dreyfus was forced to undergo a humiliating 'cashiering' ceremony in front of a crowd before being shipped to

The 1885 funeral of the great hero of the left, Victor Hugo. Alongside the pomp and ceremony was drunkenness and debauchery: prostitutes reportedly worked for free in Hugo's honour.

J'ACCUSE!

Émile Zola's *J'Accuse!* famously blamed the army for a cover-up in its conviction of Alfred Dreyfus. This led to Zola's own trial for libel, which ended in a sentence of 3000 francs and a year's imprisonment. Dreyfus himself was only cleared of any wrongdoing in 1906.

'We are horrified by the terrible light the Dreyfus affair has cast upon it all, this human sacrifice of an unfortunate man, a "dirty Jew." Ah, what a cesspool of folly and foolishness, what preposterous fantasies, what corrupt police tactics, what inquisitorial, tyrannical practices! What petty whims of a few higher-ups trampling the nation under their boots, ramming back down their throats the people's cries for truth and justice, with the travesty of state security as a pretext… It is a crime to lie to the public, to twist public opinion to insane lengths in the service of the vilest death-dealing machinations. It is a crime to poison the minds of the meek and the humble, to stoke the passions of reactionism and intolerance, by appealing to that odious anti-Semitism that, unchecked, will destroy the freedom-loving France of the Rights of Man. It is a crime to exploit patriotism in the service of hatred, and it is, finally, a crime to ensconce the sword as the modern god, whereas all science is toiling to achieve the coming era of truth and justice.' (Émile Zola, *J'Accuse!*, translated by Alexander Gray)

RIGHT: Zola's *J'Accuse!* generated a widespread public response to the Dreyfus Affair and resulted in the author's arrest for libel.

Devil's Island to serve life imprisonment for espionage. A few years later, Colonel Georges Picquart discovered that Dreyfus' letter was in fact a forgery and that a captain called Ferdinand Esterhazy was guilty of the crime. However, rather than accept the evidence, admit its error, and jail Esterhazy, the army instead imprisoned Picquart.

The Dreyfus Affair divided Paris at all levels of society, and exposed many as anti-Semites. A heated debate ensued in the press about France's identity as a Catholic nation or a republic founded on equal rights for all citizens. One of the many intellectuals arguing for equal rights was Émile Zola. Zola famously published an open letter, '*J'Accuse!*', in Georges Clemenceau's *L'Aurore* newspaper, which railed against anti-Semitism and Dreyfus' farcical trial. In response, Zola received a series of death threats and was forced to flee France for England to escape imprisonment for libel.

The Anarchists Attack

The Dreyfus Affair exposed not only deep-seated racism at the heart of Parisian society, but also the continuing power of the state to override law and terrorize its citizens. This was shown to great effect with the brutal suppression of the protests of the poor. A new breed of conservative republicans made up the majority of the National Assembly in the late nineteenth century, and their hatred of socialism was laid bare when they ordered violent police reprisals against striking workers.

For the Parisian working classes, the Belle Époque was a middle-class affair that seemed wholly uninterested in the city's poor; life for them was as difficult as ever. So while the middle classes soaked up the riverside ambience and champagne nightlife, the working classes bubbled and seethed.

Meanwhile, conservative members of the Assembly were terrified that another Commune would rise suddenly from the growing working-class discontent. Their concerns seemed confirmed when an anarchist bombed the homes of a judge and a prosecuting attorney. Both had been involved in the harsh sentencing of a group

BELOW: Here, an illustration from Parisian newspaper *Le Petit Journal* shows anarchists provoking a fight at the Pavillon d'Armenonville.

Le Petit Journal
SUPPLÉMENT ILLUSTRÉ
Huit pages : CINQ centimes

TOUS LES JOURS
Le Petit Journal
5 Centimes

TOUS LES VENDREDIS
Le Supplément illustré
5 Centimes

Troisième Année   SAMEDI 19 NOVEMBRE 1892   Numéro 104

La Dynamite à Paris

of May Day protesters, a demonstration that had ended in violence after mounted police charged the crowd. The bomber was sent to the guillotine, but many working-class Parisians considered him to be a hero and a martyr for the cause.

Soon afterwards, another bomb was delivered to a mining company office whose workers were out on strike. Five policemen were killed when the suspicious parcel blew up while being inspected. Anarchists were now the new terror to sweep Paris, and their seemingly random acts of violence were intended to blow away the capitalist and social order and create new, autonomous Communes in their place.

Nervousness quickly turned to fear when a young anarchist called Auguste Vaillant threw a bomb into the National Assembly's Chamber of Deputies, injuring several politicians. Vaillant went to the guillotine crying 'Death to bourgeois society! Long live anarchy!' This memorable martyrdom resonated not only with the disaffected working classes, but also various members of the far right who hated the government, including conservative Catholics, anti-Semites and royalists. The left had its own sympathizers: the poet Stéphane Mallarmé and the artist Camille Pissarro were both attracted to the theory of anarchy as giving a voice to the powerless.

In response to the terror, the police sought new powers to stop the anarchists. A law was passed forbidding the printing of anarchist doctrine, and all 'associations of evil-doers' were made illegal. As police spies desperately tried to infiltrate well-known anarchist haunts around the tough working-class neighbourhoods of Belleville and Ménilmontant, another spate of bomb attacks rocked the city.

The first bomb went off at the popular Café Terminus near the Gare Saint-Lazare, killing one and injuring 20 others. Another exploded in the Rue Saint-Jacques, killing a pedestrian. A third bomb accidentally went off in an anarchist's pocket as he entered the L'église de la Madeleine church, and a fourth bomb blinded a patron at the Restaurant Foyot.

The man accused of both the Café Terminus bombing and that of the mining company was Émile Henry. After being sentenced to the guillotine for killing innocent people, Henry told the judge 'there are no innocent bourgeois'. Henry had certainly been inspired by the most famous anarchist bomber, François Claudius Koenigstein, commonly known as Ravachol. Ravachol was a street brawler who became involved in the anarchist movement following

ABOVE: An 1892 illustration from *Le Petit Journal* shows the violent death of a policeman during an anarchist bombing.

OPPOSITE: Here, *Le Petit Journal* reports on the arrest of anarchist Emile Henry following the Gare Saint-Lazare bombing. Henry went to the guillotine for the crime.

The Eiffel Tower during the 1900 Universal Exposition. The tower's construction for the 1889 Exposition had both amazed and angered Parisians.

the suppression of the Paris Commune. The legend of Ravachol was perhaps somewhat bigger than the man himself: he was responsible for five deaths and the attempted murder of several magistrates. The anarchist's name, however, inspired a song and a new verb: *ravacholer*; to 'wipe out an enemy'.

In the end, the anarchist threat fizzled out in the late 1890s and the Assembly could breathe once more. It tried to dispel the notion of a divided republic with nationalism and entertainment, an Exposition celebrating the great cultural and industrial achievements of France. It was something of a gamble. The previous exposition of 1889 had both amazed and angered Parisians by building the Eiffel Tower, a monument variously criticized as 'a suppository' and 'metal asparagus' by local artists and intellectuals. Intended to mark the French Revolution's centenary, the tower was only meant to be a temporary structure and given a 20-year residence. However, attitudes to the tower changed as it stood sentinel over the 1900 Exposition; civic pride swelled and Parisians began to see their city as the cultural centre of the world.

'Parisians began to see their city as the cultural centre of the world.'

There were good reasons to turn a fresh page and leave the nineteenth century behind. There was also a lot to be proud of among the exhibits, which included

LA RAVACHOLE

A popular refrain in working-class Parisian faubourgs in the 1890s, 'La Ravachole' was sung to the tune of 'La Carmagnole':
'In the great city of Paris,
There are well-fed bourgeois,
There are the poor,
Who have an empty stomach:
The former are greedy,
Long live the sound, long live the sound,
The former are greedy,
Long live the sound
Of the explosion!...
We'll blow up all the bourgeois
We'll blow them up!
There are sell out magistrates,
There are big-bellied financiers,
There are cops,
But for all these scoundrels,
There's dynamite,
Long live the sound, long live the sound,
Of the explosion!'
(*La Ravachole*, translated by Mitch Abidor)

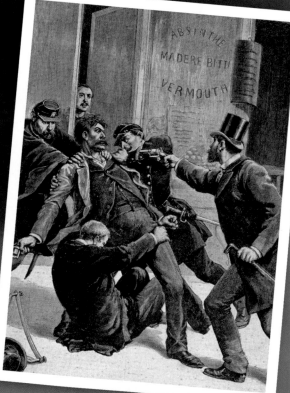

ABOVE: Henry told the judge: 'there are no innocent bourgeois.'

APACHE ARTICLE

This anonymous article from the 1905 *National Police Gazette* sums up the public mood towards the capital's Apaches:

'In Paris, that model city, well policed by the gendarmes, there are streets that are less safe than the streets of any city in the world. And that is because of the audacious Parisian thug. Fifteen years ago the songs of the toughs of Paris were so new to the public that they made a hit. They dealt with the then unknown under-life of the "eccentric" quarters; the scarcely policed fortification and the suburbs beyond them, and to the Parisians it was all extraordinary and far off. Today the ruffians have come to the centre of the capital… the Place de la Bastille was the scene of a veritable pitched battle between them and the police that surpassed anything heretofore dreamed of. In the Rue de la Roquette some twenty toughs were fighting together with knives and pistols – two bands, one against the other. Eight policemen, requisitioned by the frightened shopkeepers, tried to separate them.

Then what always happens, happened. The thugs at once forgot their personal differences to make common cause against the "agents" and one explanation of their insolent daring is found in a really too humane police regulation. While the toughs use knives and pistols freely, the police may draw their revolvers and sword bayonets only in the last extremity… for a full hour the Place de la Bastille in central Paris was a bloody battleground on which the police did the bleeding. From a dozen tough bars came reinforcements to the Apaches, as the toughs delight to call themselves, and the name has stuck…. Of the eight original policemen six were finally carried to the St. Antoine Hospital, and all with bullets somewhere in them; and the battle would have ended in the triumph of the toughs had not policemen off-duty, plain clothes men, detective inspectors, soldiers and firemen come to the rescue. Nine wounded Apaches were left on the ground by the fleeing bands.' (*National Police Gazette*, 21 October 1905)

RIGHT: A policeman shoots an Apache during a spate of inner-city violence and trouble-making.

diesel engines, escalators and talking films. One of the grand glass and iron Exhibition buildings was even lit by more than 5000 small electric light bulbs, a breathtaking night time attraction. Electric lighting transformed the city, throwing a magic new light upon the pleasures of ease and consumerism. Captivating sights included the Bon Marché department store and various fashion houses; the Pathé Cinema at the Invalides; the Paris metro; an explosion of cafés and restaurants along the city's boulevards; and glitzy, cultured and risqué nightlife that included everything from operettas to the cancan at the Moulin Rouge cabaret. There was even a new city sewer, an engineering miracle that also served as a tourist attraction.

Under the official optimism was a seedy underworld of crime and prostitution centred around Montmartre and Belleville and spreading out into new, outlying slums known as banlieues. Typically the domain of immigrants and the working poor forced by rising rents out of the city proper, the banlieues became a breeding ground for poverty and discontent that had flourished for centuries in the central city area. Violent street gangs known as Apaches, who wore red scarves and carried knives, took out their frustrations on vulnerable members of the middle class.

Armed with the 'Apache revolver' – a pistol mounted with a flick-knife and foldover brass knuckle-duster – the Apaches became the scourge of Paris' streets in the early 1900s. One Apache would seize the victim from the front while another garroted them from behind. More terrifyingly still, the Apaches seemed intent on carrying out their crimes in the wealthy centre of Paris, far from their own neighbourhoods.

The street fights between rival Apaches were a portent of similar twenty-first-century attacks by disaffected youths from the modern banlieues. However, during the Apache years of the early 1900s, the banlieues became popularly associated with the so-called second industrial revolution, largely brought on in Paris by the burgeoning automobile industry.

This created a shift in the skillset of industrial workers. Those involved in the textile boom of France's first industrial revolution were replaced by unskilled factory labourers associated with mechanized production. As the automobile, iron and chemical industries built their factories outside the city proper, but close to the banlieues, this added to a growing proletariat in these areas. The journalist Octave Mirbeau once described the banlieues as lacking identity: '[it] is no longer the city but is not yet the countryside. Nothing ends and nothing starts here.' Others grimly noted the great contrast between the glory of Paris' architecture compared with the grey and soulless apartment blocks built for the poor.

ABOVE: The Apache revolver, a three-in-one weapon that could be easily concealed in a pocket. To prevent accidental discharges while hidden, the chamber was often left empty. The pistol was lethal when fired at close range.

Divided Capital

The rise of the Apaches symbolized the growing political divisions within Paris. In many ways the city was reverting to a policy of 'them' and 'us', with 'them' not only being the working classes, but also immigrants, Jews and other foreigners. This was symptomatic of a broader trend taking place across Europe at the time. France, like all European powers of the late nineteenth century, had been involved in the European scramble for African colonies. The colonial superpowers claimed their superior technologies were the products of higher intelligence.

ABOVE: An illustration of right-wing politician Paul Déroulède stirring up nationalistic sentiment on the streets of Paris.

The notion of European racial superiority had been on display at the 1889 Exhibition, where brightly dressed African chieftains and tribespeople acted as curiosities from the 'dark continent'. Similar themes were present in the 1900 Exhibition, where a sociological display, 'The Exhibit of African American Negroes', was organized by American lawyer Thomas Calloway, who explained it would 'do a great and lasting good in convincing thinking people of the possibilities of the Negro'. Meanwhile, French atrocities against the indigenous people of Algeria seemed to contradict the idea that 'men are born and remain free and equal in rights', as the revolutionaries in France had proclaimed more than 100 years earlier.

In Paris schools, pupils were taught the latest European scientific research claiming that black people were inferior to whites. Paris could boast the Nobel-winning scientists Pierre Curie and his Polish wife Marie, but there was a wide mistrust of foreigners in the city. This was in part to do with the nationalism sweeping the continent, and was not only confined to France: Otto von Bismarck, for example, had justified his annexation of Alsace-Lorraine during the Franco–Prussian War on the grounds that its inhabitants were German 'by race'.

In Paris, opinion was not all one way, however. The Dreyfus Affair showed how fractured Parisian society had become, and also how deeply rooted its prejudices lay. The fragmentation of opinion was shown in the election of 1898, which produced a government of 80 Royalists, 74 Radical Socialists, 254 moderate Republicans, 57 Socialists, 15 Nationalists and 4 well-known anti-Semites. This problem of Parisian and French national identity was also increasingly caught up in the troubled role of the Church.

The Catholic Church, under increasing attack from Darwinism and agnostic socialism, had remained conspicuously aloof during the Dreyfus Affair. Catholic opinion had been buoyed by the new Assumptionist newspaper *La Croix*, which stood defiantly against the socialists and anti-clerical republicans who had defended Dreyfus. Together with the royalists and high-ranking members of the army – who had been educated by Jesuits – the Catholics promoted the nationalistic view of the French 'race', as opposed to the republican notion that all people represented humanity.

This new right-wing nationalism had bite, but the republicans had the numbers in government. In response to a coup led by the nationalistic politician Paul Déroulède, the republicans created the Radical Socialist party and the French Socialist Party, led by Jean Jaurès, to form a left-wing government. Its first point of order was to ban *La Croix* and the Assumptionist order and start separating Church from State.

From then on, the State would not pay Church salaries – for any denomination – or allow the Church to play any role in the provision of education. The freedom to worship, however, was written into law. So, nearly five centuries after the destructive Wars of Religion and over a century after the French Revolution had come and gone, the new republican government had turned France into a secular nation.

The Great War

For many Parisians, the advent of World War I came as a shock, despite the obvious diplomatic tensions that had been mounting between the European superpowers. Two assassinations in 1914 tipped the balance and alerted Paris to the impending danger. The first was of Austrian Archduke Franz Ferdinand in Sarajevo by Serbian anarchist Gavrilo Princip, the event that infamously began the mobilization of Europe's troops. Austria-Hungary and its ally Germany declared war on Serbia; Russia, the traditional defender of Serbia, along with its allies France and Britain, then declared war on Austria-Hungary.

The second assassination was of Jean Jaurès, the socialist leader, who had pleaded with the Chamber of Deputies not to blindly follow Russia into a conflict with Germany. 'Are we going to start a world war?' Jaurès demanded of his parliament. It was the sentence that would seal his fate. On 31 July, Jaurès was shot in the back by a young nationalist fanatic while dining at the Café du Croissant. This in turn allowed Paris' sabre-rattling nationalists to step into the void left by Jaurès. But it was too late for oratory, from either side. War had arrived.

'For many Parisians, the advent of World War I came as a shock.'

BELOW: The funeral of socialist leader Jean Jaurés following his assassination by a nationalist fanatic. Jaurés policy of Franco-German rapprochement made him a hated figure among French nationalists.

Refugees arrive at the Gare de Lyon after the German shelling of Belgium. The heavy howitzers had made short work of the Belgian fortifications.

Paris awoke when Austria-Hungary invaded Serbia; suddenly war fever swept the city. Parisian men began signing up in great numbers, including the 70-year-old writer Anatole France and various others who were not fit for service; shop signs written in German were vandalized; hundreds of the city's citizens flocked to see its soldiers set off from the Gare du Nord. The sounds of military tunes filled the air: the boys from the City of Light were off to smash the Boches and win back Alsace-Lorraine for the republic. The newspapers predicted a quick victory: the troops would be back in time for Christmas.

The excitement and flag waving died down as the city became all but deserted. Theatres, shops and cafés closed at 8 p.m., and the City of Light became the City of Darkness as official blackouts took effect. Zeppelins dropping bombs were now joined by the first bomber planes known; the harm to the city was minimal, but the psychological damage of death from above was great. News of those casualties that did occur – two were killed and 19 injured during raids – became

PROCLAMATIONS OF RETREAT

On 3 September 1914, two proclamations were made to the Parisian public. The first was by the government:

'In order to watch over the national welfare, it is the duty of the public powers to remove themselves temporarily from the city of Paris. Under the command of an eminent Chief, a French Army, full of courage and zeal, will defend the capital and its patriotic population against the invader… At the request of the military authorities, the Government is therefore temporarily transferring its headquarters to a place where it can remain in constant touch with the whole of the country…It knows that it does not need to recommend to the admirable population of Paris that calm, resolution, and coolness which it is showing every day, and which is on a level with its highest traditions.'

The second proclamation, made by Gallieni, was rather less inspirational in tone:

'ARMY OF PARIS, INHABITANTS OF PARIS,
The members of the Government of the Republic have left Paris to give a fresh impulse to national defence.
I have been entrusted with the task of defending Paris against the invader.
That task I will fulfill to the end.
GALLIENI, Commandant of the Army of Paris'

RIGHT: Joseph Gallieni was brought out of retirement to become Commander of the Army of Paris.

permanently embargoed. However, German planes provided their own news, such as dropping leaflets announcing French army defeats.

On the front, the French troops found themselves trapped somewhere between the warfare of Napoleon and that of the modern age. There seemed to be a notion that the high morale and spirit of the French troops would in itself be enough to undo the might of the matching German army. But they were badly under-equipped. In weaponry, for example, France had only 310 heavy artillery guns, compared with the Germans' 3600. The French brass had dismissed the idea of introducing the machine gun only a few years earlier, but the weapon would destroy their troops in the opening battles of the war. Even the French uniforms were from a bygone era: the bright blue kepi hats, jackets and red trousers made the French troops sitting ducks for the modern German soldiers dressed in battlefield grey. The methodology of war had changed too. Lines of French troops and cavalry officers, swords raised high and breastplates glinting in the sun, charged for up to a 1.6km (1 mile) into the German lines. Here, German machine guns mowed them down en masse.

There were reports of another terrifying new German weapon, described as the most powerful gun ever invented. Designed in secret over the years building up to the war, the Krupp 'Big Bertha' heavy howitzer could fire an 800kg (1760lb) shell over a staggering 13km (8-mile) range. Each shell was also fitted with a time-delay fuse, delaying the explosion until it had penetrated an enemy fortress. Thirty-six horses were needed to tow a Big Bertha; two of the guns made short

ABOVE: 'Big Bertha' was the largest gun ever constructed and the secret behind the rapid destruction of the Belgian defences.

ABOVE: **Parisians here come out to watch German aircraft drop bombs on the city. Aeroplanes at that time were still something of a novelty.**

work of the allegedly impregnable Belgium fortresses along the country's border. With the Belgian defences destroyed, the Germans pushed with alarming speed towards France and Paris.

The Belgian refugees streaming into Paris brought the reality of war into the capital; Big Bertha compounded the terror within the city. A German plane killed two with a bomb on the Canal Saint-Martin and dropped leaflets that read 'There is nothing you can do but surrender.' Then, suddenly, German cavalry riders were sighted on the outskirts of the city.

Paris was now in a panic. The veteran commander Joseph-Simon Gallieni was brought out of retirement to protect the city. Gallieni was brutally honest about its prospects. Privately, he had told the government that Paris could not hold out against the Germans and that it should leave the capital immediately with the Bank of France's gold reserves. As they carried out this suggestion, War Minister Alexandre Millerand explained to Gallieni tersely that he expected the capital to be defended 'à outrance'. This meant destroying the city's buildings and bridges and defending it to the last man. Gallieni later recorded that the expectation was that he was being left behind to die.

The departing government sought to bolster Parisian confidence by confiding that 'The Government leaves Paris only after having assured the defence of the city and of the entrenched camp by every means in its power.' Nothing could have been further from the truth. Paris was wide open and the government and Gallieni knew it. The fortifications built by Adolphe Thiers were in a state of disrepair and there were so many refugees in Paris that its food supply would not last under siege for longer than three weeks. Worse still, there was not even an army to defend the capital. Gallieni had insisted that he needed three fresh divisions to have any chance of withstanding a German siege, but those sent by Commander in Chief Joseph Joffre were instead a disordered and exhausted remnant sent back from the front.

The city fell into hysteria, with a panicked exodus by those who could leave and desperate hoarding by those who couldn't. Great numbers of sheep and cattle were brought into the city, as many remembered the rat pies of the last German siege in 1870. There were also outbreaks of violence, as refugees with accents were accused of being German spies. Machine-gun nests were thrown up around key buildings such as Notre Dame and the Eiffel Tower. Trees were removed to provide clear lines of fire for the city's 3000 small artillery cannons, and bridges prepared for immediate demolition if the city's defences failed. With morale low, many prayed to Saint Geneviève, the saviour of the city from Attila, imploring her once more for protection from the Huns.

'Millerand explained tersely that he expected the capital to be defended à outrance.'

The Miracle of the Marne

If Saint Geneviève did provide divine help, perhaps it was in the shape of the so-called 'Miracle of the Marne'. This was a bloodied map discovered on the corpse of a German officer detailing the plan of the German attack. It showed that the German army did not intend a direct invasion of Paris, but would first drop south of the city and then move east, attacking the French forces stationed on the border with Switzerland. Crucially, this would leave a whole flank of the German army exposed to the northeast of Paris: it was here that Gallieni decided to attack with the full might of his reserves.

The problem for Gallieni was supply: he had no way of actually getting his men to the Germans marching just south of the river of Marne. Then he struck

BELOW: Gallieni requisitioned 600 Renault taxis, popularly known after 1914 as the 'Taxi de la Marne', to deliver his men to Marne. Two can be seen at the back of this line.

on an ingenious solution: he would transport his troops by taxi. So it was that the capital's 600-strong fleet of taxis was employed to deliver the protectors of Paris, with five to a car, to fight the Battle of the Ourcq at Marne. For many soldiers, the 60km (37 miles) to Marne was their first ride in an automobile, and it did not come cheap. The government was charged full fare for each round trip to Marne, a cost of around 70,000 francs. At the sight of the red Renault taxis ferrying more than 6000 soldiers to the front, Gallieni was famously heard to remark: 'Eh bien, voilà au moins qui n'est pas banal!' ('Well, here at least is something out of the ordinary!')

Gallieni's efforts at Marne, in combination with Joffre's forces and that of the British Expeditionary Force, created a great German retreat that turned the early tide of the war. However, it also came at a great cost: of 250,000 French casualties, 80,000 had been killed. The Germans reported similar losses. Marne ended German hopes of a fast and decisive victory; it also preceded a bleak and bloody four years of trench warfare along the Western front stretching from the English Channel to Switzerland. Paris would remain throughout a city at war.

Everyday Life

After Marne, calm fell over Paris and local lives went back to something resembling normality. Theatres reopened, concerts were given, dancing, music and café culture again became the mainstay of the capital's life. There were restrictions: croissants and brioches were banned for a time, and local officials recommended each family have one dinner a week without.

BELOW: French soldiers on leave from the front. Paris during World War I became the centre for military rest and recuperation: it was a world away from the horrors of the trenches.

MATA HARI

The most famous spy of World War I was a Dutch woman, Margaretha Zelle, better known as Mata Hari. The mistress of the French industrialist Émile Guimet, Zelle was a society girl who had worked as an exotic dancer and a horseback rider in the circus before marrying. Zelle began selling secrets to the Germans at the outbreak of war, often travelling to the German embassy in Madrid to deliver her reports. French intelligence caught wind of Zelle by intercepting messages from the Madrid embassy, which referred to an agent called H-21. By making Zelle privy to false military information that was then transmitted from the Madrid embassy, French intelligence were able to confirm that H-21 was Zelle. She was convicted of espionage and executed by firing squad in the moat of the Château de Vincennes on 15 October 1917.

RIGHT: Before she became one of the most infamous spies of wartime Europe, Mata Hari performed as a professional dancer under the name of Lady MacLeod.

It was a far cry from the siege of 1870, and Paris adopted a rather pleased-with-itself attitude. Although the war was being fought only 240km (150 miles) from the city, the only real evidence of the fighting came in the form of shell-shocked soldiers on rest and recuperation from the horrors of the trenches. Refugees and immigrants also flocked to Paris. Immigrants from the French colonies, including Africa and Indo-China were drafted in to work in the munitions and tank factories, so native Parisians could travel to the front. Foreigners, for the most part, were treated with great suspicion.

Nationalistic feeling flourished, with Germans vilified as 'barbarians', 'baby-killers', 'sexual deviants' and 'cannibals'. Espionage was a threat to Paris both real and imagined; foreigners were often accused of spying. Nationalism and the war, on the other hand, also had a unifying effect on French-speaking Parisians; for the first time in many years class resentments did not show. This solidarity, however, would not last for long.

In 1917, a great wave of discontent swept France. The army suffered several mutinies at the front, and Parisians were becoming fed up with the seemingly endless conflict. There was political unrest too, as the cost of living mounted and Parisian workers demanded compensation for their sacrifice. In May, strikes broke out among women clothing workers; the trouble then spread to banks, restaurants, factories and other industries. In most instances the demands for more money were granted, but some strike leaders were jailed for hindering the war effort.

ABOVE: Here, the destruction wrought by the *Luftstreitkräfte's* new Gotha bombers is shown. The planes were a military marvel at a time when Zeppelins were commonly employed to drop missiles.

The veteran statesman Georges Clemenceau was elected prime minister on a platform of calming tensions and bringing an end to the war. Paris once again became the target of German aerial bombardment. The Russians had dropped out of the war to fight their revolution, and now Germany was free to focus all of its attention on the Western Front. In January 1918, the German *Luftstreitkräfte* (air force) dispatched four squadrons of brand new Gotha bombers, which dropped more than 200 missiles on the suburbs of Paris.

The attacks continued throughout March and Parisians sought shelter in the city's underground metro stations. But here too, there was destruction and 60 Parisians were crushed to death trying to enter the crammed Bolivar station.

The Paris Gun

The Germans had not yet unleashed their most terrible weapon, a long-range cannon designed for the specific task of destroying the capital, called simply the 'Paris Gun'. Also designed by Krupp, the manufacturer of the Big Bertha, the Paris Gun fired a one-tonne shell from a 34m-long (111ft) barrel to a distance of 130km (81 miles) and an altitude of 42km (26 miles), the greatest height achieved by a missile before the Nazi V2 rocket. Weighing more than 230 tonnes, the Paris Gun could only be moved along railway tracks and was first set up in the forests of Coucy, around 112km (70 miles) from Paris.

Parisians reported feeling surprise during the start of what was to be 140 days of shelling. With no Zeppelins or planes flying overhead, it was if the shells had come from nowhere. The first shell to claim lives landed on the Quai de la Seine, killing eight and injuring another dozen. The Germans, however, had little control over what the Paris Gun hit. It was almost always aimed at the Louvre, but not one shell struck this target. When it did hit a building, however, the gun's destructive capabilities were evident. One fateful Sunday, a single shell landed on the church of Saint-Gervais during mass, killing 75. The Paris Gun would not be enough to change Germany's fortunes in the war. With the support of their new allies the Americans, the British forces finally broke through the German lines at the beginning of August 1918. By October, the German army had been all but destroyed. On 11 November, the Great War ended.

Paris took on a festival atmosphere in the days following the armistice, but with time and reflection few could celebrate the consequences of the war. As the soldiers returned from the trenches, thin and bedraggled, many convalesced in the buildings constructed for the 1900 Exhibition. Once these glass and iron structures had dazzled the world with their thousands of electric lights, one of the great industrial achievements of the modern age. Now, the Exhibition buildings were covered in the dust and grime of war, and once proud Parisian men lay broken on stretchers inside. More than 1.4 million Frenchmen had lost their lives, the largest loss of life during a conflict by any single nation in history. Then, as if mocking the numbers of the war dead, the Spanish Flu pandemic of 1918 claimed nearly 1800 Parisians in one week.

It was impossible to imagine that the four years between 1914 and 1918 could ever be repeated. They were, of course, only a prelude to a far more devastating conflict to come, a war that would expose the fragility of a European peace and the inability of its leaders to prevent an aggressor. World War II would bring out the worst and the best in the people of Paris, casting a long shadow over the City of Light. Global slaughter snuffed out the dreams and promises of the Belle Époque.

BELOW: Two men urge Parisians to adopt face masks against the deadly Spanish Flu pandemic, which swept through the capital in 1918 following the end of World War I.

WAR AND PEACE

Paris emerged from the war battered and scarred, its people bitterly divided. As xenophobia and anti-Semitism rose to the surface, the city's revolutionary ideals of liberty, equality and fraternity would undergo their sternest test. Meanwhile, France's enemy amassed its armies; this time no-one would protect Paris from the German peril.

PARIS IN THE 1920s and 30s was a city mired in its fear of foreigners. Russians, Poles, Armenians, North Africans and Italians escaping Mussolini's fascist regime all settled in Paris in the 1920s, as did Jews from many different nations. This was a necessary part of repopulating Paris; the city had lost tens of thousands of its men in the war, and the new influx of foreigners filled the void. Before the war, foreigners had made up only 5 per cent of the capital's population; by 1930, it was 9.2 per cent. Many Parisians regarded this as an invasion.

Foreigners were called *métèques*, a pejorative term for immigrants first used by nationalist poet Charles Maurras during the Dreyfus Affair. During the 1930s, *métèques* were blamed for all of Paris' maladies: rising crime levels, unemployment, even the city's broken economy following the 1929 Wall Street Crash. Many called for 'La France aux Français!' ('France for the French!'), and violence against foreigners became a regular occurrence.

Anti-Semitism was also on the rise, even among those on the left who expounded the virtues of the 1789 Revolution. The communist newspaper

OPPOSITE: 14 June 1940: the day the French capital became a city of the Third Reich. Seven days later, Hitler made his one and only visit to Paris.

De la Roque led marching protesters on 6 February 1936 to the Place de la Concorde, where they faced off against armed police and rival protesters from the left. Violence quickly erupted. Shots were fired into the crowd, mounted police initiated charges, and a running battle ensued. It was the closest a rioting mob had been to overthrowing the government since 1870, but in the end the police were able to restore order. Of 40,000 protesters, 16 were killed and 600 wounded, and 1000 policemen were injured.

Despite its many supporters, the right was not able to bring about revolution. Instead, the left fought back by forming a coalition, known as the Front Populaire, between the Socialist Party's Léon Blum and the Communist Party's Maurice Thorez. After a 500,000-strong general strike by Front Populaire members, the party swept into power during a landslide 1936 election. As cries went out of 'Vive le Front Populaire' and 'Vive la Commune', it seemed like workers' revolution had finally arrived and a commune could be achieved. But it was an illusion. Workers' rights briefly improved under the Front Populaire, but before long there were lengthy strikes, rising inflation, and an economy that seemed in free fall. And then, in 1939, the world changed forever.

World War II

There was nothing unusual about the Parisian summer of 1939, the 150th anniversary of the French Revolution. In domestic politics, the Front Populaire had peaked in popularity and the franc was still steadily declining; a German

TRIFLES FOR A MASSACRE

Novelist Louis-Ferdinand Céline, a violent anti-Semite, expressed common prejudices about Jews at the time of the Stavisky Affair in his snarling diatribe *Trifles for a Massacre*:

'During the entire Stavisky Affair one word of order was passed to every editorial room around the world, a formal commission, which must have cost dearly every day... That little Jewish paranoiac could have been called a Turk, a perfidious foreigner, a half-breed, an oriental spy, a Polish adventurer, a hairdresser, a dentist, a parachutist, a pimp, a syphilitic, a Newfoundlander, a deracinated person... anything whatever... for the sake of evasion, diversion... but never the proper noun JEW... He could have been anything but that... He would never have been able to survive all of his travails save for the influence of Jewry... The Jews do not reveal their chiefs... They weave their web in the shadows... They exhibit only their puppets... their entertainers, their "stars." The Jewish passion, so unanimous, so shadowy, is the passion of the termite. In the march of these insects, all of the obstacles become weakened, ruined, and matted back together little by little, unto the very fiber... ignobly resolute in the most foul, shitty magma of rotten juice and mandibles... unto the final calamity, the total collapse, into the Jewish void.' (Louis-Ferdinand Céline, *Trifles for a Massacre*, translated by Mary Hudson)

serial killer was guillotined before an eager crowd, the last to suffer this form of capital punishment in public; and the French translation of Margaret Mitchell's *Gone With The Wind* hit bookshelves in time for summer vacations.

Then, on 1 September, Hitler invaded Poland. The strategy of appeasement adopted by France and Britain after the failure of the Treaty of Versailles now reached its ignominious end: the Allies declared war on Germany. After the initial shock had settled in, Parisians went back to their everyday lives. The Paris spring of 1940 was one of the warmest on record; a soporific air descended over the capital.

There were some signs that the country was at war: a 10 p.m. curfew was in place; there were alcohol-free days; *pâtisseries* were only open three days a week, and rationing was allegedly in place for the soldiers guarding the Maginot Line. The Line was an immense chain of concrete fortifications and gun installations connected by underground tunnels that ran from France's Swiss border to Belgium. Although in World War I the Germans had previously entered France via Belgium, the Maginot Line was not built along this border. This was apparently a diplomatic gesture to avoid upsetting the neutral ally of Belgium, but also so that any possible battle with Germany would take place on Belgian rather than French soil.

Many members of the French military, including Colonel Charles de Gaulle, felt this strategy to be flawed. Simply, it was based on the premise that World War II would be fought along the same grounds as World War I; that

ABOVE: Right-wing demonstrators set fire to a kiosk after marching through the streets during a 1936 protest over the Stavisky Affair.

OPPOSITE: This propaganda poster published by the anti-Semitic newspaper *La Libre Parole* warns of the Jewish threat to French society. Founded in 1892, the newspaper gained popular support after the Dreyfus Affair.

ABOVE: French conscripts gather at the recruitment station at Paris' Gare de l'Est in 1939, eager to set off for war.

is, a war of attrition fought between long lines of opposing trenches. However, Hitler had shown as early as 1937, during his brutal bombing of the Spanish town of Guernica, that he did not have trench warfare in mind. Hitler's war would instead be fought according to blitzkrieg: his highly mobile armies would be led by panzers and protected by the Luftwaffe; invasion would be brutal, fast and efficient, and over before the Allies could muster a coherent retaliation.

So it was that, in May, Nazi divisions pushed fearlessly through Holland and Belgium and into France. Paris prepared itself by digging trenches, removing the stained glass from Sainte-Chapelle, and packing and cataloguing important artworks from the Louvre, sending some away in trucks to the Loire Valley. Then, in June, after an earlier promise to stay in the capital and several days of bombing by the Luftwaffe, the French government fled Paris, leaving it an 'open city'. Without a standing army to protect them, Parisians panicked. A mass exodus of the city began: there was a long procession of people, cars, horses, livestock, carts, prams and whatever possessions people could carry or push before them. When the German army entered the city on 14 June, only a third of the population remained. On 17 June, Philippe Pétain, the new head of the French 'Vichy' government, made a radio announcement: 'It is with a heavy heart that I tell you today that we must cease hostilities. The fighting must stop.' On 21 June 1940, France signed an armistice with Germany. Three days later, Hitler made his one and only visit to the capital. Paris was now German.

The New City

What shocked many about the bloodless takeover of Paris was how quickly the city returned to something resembling everyday life. In the first weeks of the occupation, cafés, theatres and cinemas reopened, restaurants such as Maxim's welcomed their new clients, fashion houses went back to business; Coco Chanel herself took up residence at the Ritz with a Nazi officer. The refugees who had fled Paris began their long march back to the city, most at the Germans' behest. The Nazis themselves sequestered the city's hotels as their lodgings, raised street signs in German around the city, and hung long swastika flags from its most notable buildings. Some Parisians recorded 'open fraternization' taking place between the Germans and the capital's women.

> ‘Parisians were told what was expected of them via loudspeakers.’

The Nazis occupying Paris were on strict orders from Hitler to be on their best behaviour. His plan was to persuade the Parisians, whom he considered cowardly and degenerate, to accept his Germanization of Paris peacefully and therefore 'at several levels preserve undamaged the wonder of Western civilization'. Civilization, of course, was a matter of definition; within weeks of the occupation more than 500 Louvre artworks had been burned as immoral. Joan Miró, a resident of the city a few years earlier, was among the artists whose work was destroyed.

As part of Hitler's reorganization, Parisians were told what was expected of them via loudspeakers. A curfew would be in effect from 9 p.m. to 5 a.m. every

BELOW: Parisians flock to the Gare Montparnasse to escape the city, as the German army approaches.

Hitler's one-day tour of Paris included having his photo taken at popular landmarks with architect Albert Speer (left) and artist Arno Breker (right). Hitler promised every German soldier one visit to Paris.

night. No hostility towards the Reich would be tolerated: any aggression or acts of sabotage were punishable by death. The various departments of the Reich then set up their headquarters in the city's most salubrious buildings; many high-ranking party members such as Herman Göring and Joseph Goebbels commandeered their own office space. One of the buildings was also used for the 'embassy' of the collaborating Vichy government, led by Pétain and in principle responsible for the administration outside Paris. Hated by the French and scorned by the Nazis, the Vichy government would soon be responsible for aiding the removal of the city's most undesirable residents. One of the most notorious buildings was the Gestapo's headquarters at 11 Rue des Saussaies, where screams from the interrogation chambers could be heard from the street outside.

ABOVE: The German cavalry canters down the Champs-Élysées, as the Reich takes control of the city.

The Nazis did not hide their racial policies; more surprising to the occupiers themselves was how many Parisians became willful accomplices in the persecution of the city's Jews. As the Nazi Propaganda Division of Greater Paris set up its headquarters under the watchful eye of SS officer Kurt Lischka, a violent sadist who enjoyed torture, many of the city's newspapers began espousing Nazi doctrine. Lischka, who had been responsible for the deportation of 30,000 Jews after Kristallnacht in Berlin in 1938, was now charged with solving the 'Jewish problem' in Paris. He led the deportation and subsequent murder of 80,000 French Jews; 43,000 of them were from Paris.

Lischka began his propaganda campaign with anti-Semitic newsreels that explained to cinemagoers that France's collapse had been brought about by Jews, freemasons, communists, Romani, homosexuals, blacks, and various other *métèques*. Films such as *The Jewish Peril* and *The Corrupter* portrayed beady-eyed Jewish caricatures plotting the overthrow of European society.

Similar motifs were shown at an exhibition called 'Le Juif et la France', or 'The Jews and France', much of which was based on the work of George Montandon,

DEATH TO THE JEW

Edited by novelist Jean Drault, *Au Pilori* was a collaborationist Parisian newspaper that appealed to its readers to denounce their Jewish neighbours by sending letters to the editor or to the authorities. This stance was made possible by the Vichy government's repeal of the April 1939 Marchandeau decree that prohibited anti-Semitism in the press. Only one of a number of popular Parisian daily and weekly newspapers that supported the persecution of Jews, *Au Pilori* was the first to suggest that 'The Jewish Question must be resolved immediately by the arrest and deportation of all Jews without exception.' The following text is from a 1941 edition of *Au Pilori*, which appeared under the headline 'Death to the Jew':

'Death to the Jew! Death to all that is false, ugly, dirty, repulsive, Negroid, cross-bred, Jewish!... For the Jew is not a man. He is a stinking beast… We defend ourselves against evil, against death – and therefore against the Jews!... Death to the Jew! Death to villainy, duplicity, to the Russian Jew! Death to the Jewish argument! Death to Jewish usury… Yes! We repeat! Let us repeat! Death! D.E.A.T.H. to the Jew!' (*Au Pilori*, 1941)

BELOW: In 1941, the Third Reich stepped up its persecution of Jews with the first round-up, shown here.

Professor of Anthropology at the School of Paris and author of an article titled 'How to recognize a Jew?' Visited by more than 200,000 people, the general theme of the exhibition was to reveal the corrupting influence of Jews on French life, including the military, film, economics and literature. Stereotypical images of Jews were provided so viewers would be better able to recognize one in future; French Jews, it was explained, often hid away from sight in their Riviera palaces.

The Persecution Begins

Alongside the anti-Semitic propaganda in 1940 were a series of laws curbing the rights of Jews. They were prohibited from certain restaurants and public places, were not allowed to use telephones or bicycles, and could not practise as lawyers or doctors or own shops. The Vichy government joined in by setting up a commission that denaturalized more than 10,000 Jews.

The Nazi plans for Paris depended upon the active aid of the French authorities. Police carried out the first round-ups of Jews in 1941, claiming that it was aimed at 'criminals'. This followed a demonstration by young communist Parisians in August 1941, when a scuffle broke out with soldiers and shots were fired. In response, the Vichy government gave itself new powers to execute communists. Two of the organizers of the demonstration, Henri Gautherot and Samuel Tyszelman, were condemned to death and shot.

'The police had powers to arrest any Jew they found in the street.'

This, however, was only a prelude for the real reprisals. On 20 August, the Nazis ordered a round-up of Jews, saying they were responsible for the demonstration in the 11th arrondissement, a supposed hotbed of communist activity. After closing off the roads and a local metro station, 2500 Vichy policemen began arresting Jews between 18 and 50 years old listed on the Nazi *Fichier Juif*, the registration file of all Jews living in Occupied France. The police had powers to arrest any Jew they found in the street; if a name from the list could not be located, the nearest male relative could be arrested instead.

Within two days, 4230 Jewish men were arrested and transported to the town of Drancy, today a northeastern suburb of Paris. Here, an unfinished tower block intended as modern public apartments became an internment camp. Between 1942 and 1944, nearly 70,000 Jews were deported from Drancy to concentration

BELOW: The notice in this Parisian restaurant window prohibits Jews from entering.

MICHEL JACQUOT

SEPTEMBRE - OCTOBRE
EXPOSITION
LE JUIF
ET LA FRANCE
PALAIS BERLITZ, 31 B° DES ITALIENS

ABOVE: A poster for *Le Juif et la France*, or 'The Jews and France', an exhibition of anti-Semitism based on the work of French professor George Montandon.

RIGHT: Jewish prisoners are put onto trains bound for internment camps outside Paris, including Pithiviers and Beaune-la-Rolande. The most notorious camp was an unfinished tower block at Drancy.

camps around Europe. Most of them, under the secret orders of Adolf Eichmann, one of the main organizers of the Holocaust, were sent to Auschwitz concentration camp in occupied Poland.

Drancy was a harbinger of the horrors awaiting Jewish internees. The first detainees arrived in August 1941 in a highly distressed and disorientated state. Some who had been arrested at their homes had had time to pack a bag, but other less fortunate people had been taken from the street and arrived with nothing. Nor would they be properly supplied at Drancy: there were no blankets and very few mattresses; most slept on a bare concrete floor.

'Drancy was a harbinger of the horrors awaiting Jewish internees.'

The rules permitted Drancy detainees to write to their families every fortnight, but personal visitors were prohibited, as were books. There were other rules at Drancy, but as they were not written down anywhere, the prisoners only found out what they were by breaking them. The cruelty of the Vichy guards quickly became legend. Proudly anti-Semitic, the guards took pleasure in hitting inmates with truncheons, including women, who for a time were also held at Drancy. One inmate recalled a guard using his truncheon to strike a four-year-old girl so hard that she was knocked unconscious.

Another punishment was being sentenced to 'La Gnouf', or 'The Nick': a cell 3 by 4m (10 by 13ft) into which 30 inmates were crammed. There was no room to sit or lie down and only a bucket provided as a toilet. Detainees received a sentence of two days in La Gnouf for crimes such as stealing a vegetable while on kitchen duty; those caught smoking inside were given a month.

BELOW: The first Jews arrive at the internment camp at Drancy. Drancy introduced internees to methods of torture such as the roll call, which were widely employed in Nazi concentration camps.

STAR OF SOLIDARITY

The wearing of the yellow star for Paris' Jews had an oddly polarizing effect on non-Jewish inhabitants. Some were pleased the supposed enemy was out in the open, but for many it showed that Jews, so horribly caricatured in the films and the 'Le Juif et la France' exhibition, actually looked the same as them. For others, the yellow star was the antithesis of the French republican values of liberty, fraternity and equality; underground newspapers called for a movement of solidarity with anyone who wore a yellow star. Parisian Jews reported receiving supportive smiles in the street and out-of-character friendliness from strangers, while others took their support one step further and began wearing stars of their own. Wearers of these stars would often embellish them with their own words, such as 'Buddhist', 'Zulu', or 'Goy', Yiddish for 'non-Jew'. This small spark of light was quickly stamped out, however. Those caught wearing stars were arrested and punished, while others were put on transports to Drancy and never seen again.

RIGHT: From July 1942, all Parisian Jews were required to wear the yellow Star of David.

The roll call, a notorious method of torture used throughout Nazi concentration camps, was also employed at Drancy. Inmates were made to stand for hours in every type of weather while the roll was called, and then called again, depending on the mood of the guards. Attendance at the roll call was compulsory; those too sick to stand were carried out on stretchers.

All of this, one prisoner noted, would have been bearable if there had been enough to eat. In the early months of Drancy, detainees were given a daily ration of two small bowls of clear soup, 150g (5oz) of bread and 200g (7oz) of unpeeled vegetables. The portions would become more meagre as the war went on, and death from starvation became commonplace.

One of the most zealously enforced rules at Drancy was that prohibiting looking out a window when SS captain Theodor Dannecker was visiting. Eichmann had personally employed 27-year-old Dannecker to oversee the Final Solution in Paris after being impressed by the captain's ruthless determination to exterminate Jews. While it had been Kurt Lischka's job to assure Parisians that they needed to be rid of their Jews, it was up to Dannecker to actually carry this out. Dannecker called his plan to round up and deport 28,000 of the city's Jews

ABOVE: Internees at Drancy carry out their washing with the facilities made available to them.

'Spring Wind', and he hoped it would provide a prototype that could be used in other European cities of the Reich.

The round-up in August 1941 was only a first step in Dannecker's plan, who apparently became irritated by the small numbers of Jews that could be interned at Drancy. He was further annoyed by the release of several hundred Drancy detainees by the German military on health grounds while he was in Berlin getting married. Dannecker's schedule for Spring Wind would have to be escalated.

In July 1942, new decrees concerning the rights of Jews were announced. From then on, Jews were banned from all main streets, cinemas, libraries, parks, restaurants and cafés, and were only allowed to go shopping between 3 p.m. and 4 p.m.; the Nazis knew there was little left to purchase at this hour. In addition, all children over the age of six would be required to wear a yellow Star of David on their clothing. Then Dannecker ordered another round-up. This was to involve far greater numbers than before and include women and children as well as men.

The Vél' d'Hiv Round-up

At 4 a.m. on 16 July 1942, Paris' green public buses and blue police vans made their way to those parts of the city with the highest population of Jewish residents. Carrying lists of Jews to be detained were 900 teams of French Vichy policemen, working in groups of two or three. The police had bolstered their numbers by employing thugs from the Front Populaire. The police were under strict instructions to locate and identify Jews and arrest them without taking notice of protest, argument, or state of health. If any tried to flee, armed police waiting by the transport were told to open fire, as one later recalled: 'If there was the slightest attempt to escape we were told to fire into the crowd. That's what the submachine guns were for.'

Police teams banged at front doors; others hacked them down with axes. The reaction of the victims also varied: some packed a small bag with the permitted 'blanket, sweater, pair of shoes and two shirts' and left quietly, others wailed and threw themselves around the legs of the arresting policemen pleading not to be taken. As with the 1940 round-up, if any from the list could not be found another was taken in their place. For some it was simply too much to bear; more than 100 committed suicide rather than be taken in.

Of the 13,152 arrested Jews, 7500 were interred in the Vélodrome d'Hiver cycling stadium, better known to Parisians as the Vél' d'Hiv. More joined this number until it reached 8160. Around 4000 of them were children. The rest of the Jews were taken to Drancy. This had now simply become a holding camp before deportation; prisoners either died there or were moved to a concentration camp; no one remained there for long. Of those from the 16 July round-up, 879 were bordered onto cattle trucks bound for Auschwitz on 19 July; 375 of them went directly to the gas chamber. Between 19 July and 11 November 1942, 29,878 Jews were deported from Drancy; most were murdered on arrival.

In the Vél' d'Hiv, conditions were inhuman. The 12 toilets there quickly became blocked and the detainees were forced to relieve themselves against the walls. No air flowed through the enclosed stadium, and the heat and stench soon became unbearable. The water supply had been cut off, and the only food was the watery soup delivered by the Red Cross – but there was not enough of this for everyone.

BELOW: A rare photo of those transported to the Vélodrome d'Hiver cycling stadium, after the round-up of July 1942.

Hysteria soon spread through the stadium: a Red Cross nurse reported people crammed on top of each other without room to lie down; children as well as adults cried and screamed. Some seemed to have been simply driven mad. Odd bundles of clothes were also seen falling from the grandstand, but on closer inspection these turned out to be people who had ended their lives.

The Jewish internment in the Vél' d'Hiv went on for five days. During this time babies were born, women had miscarriages, and many were brought close to death through dehydration. After a few days, a group of Paris' firemen were ordered to the Vél' d'Hiv to provide a safety check. Not sure what was expected of them, the firemen were horrified by what they found inside. Many detainees asked them for help or to post letters to their loved ones. Hundreds of letters were smuggled from the Vél' d'Hiv in this way. Some of the firemen also broke orders and turned their hoses on for the detainees, providing them with a few moments of merciful water.

> 'Ration cards were issued, but these did not guarantee food; shops were empty.'

Between 19 and 22 July, the prisoners of Vél' d'Hiv were loaded onto trains and transported to internment camps at Pithiviers and Beaune-la-Rolande, south of Paris. From here, most would be sent to Auschwitz, but even Dannecker became nervous at the idea of sending young children to the concentration camp without Eichmann's authorization. So when the camps at Pithiviers and Beaune-la-Rolande were emptied, the children stayed behind. It was the job of the Vichy guards to separate the children from their mothers. This they did with truncheons and rifle butts.

DANNECKER'S FAILURE

Spring Wind was considered a failure by the Nazis; Dannecker had prepared for 28,000 to be deported from Paris during the round-up, but had captured less than half that number. Many are thought to have caught wind of the raid and fled Paris the night before. Eichmann agreed that Dannecker had failed and he was recalled to Berlin in late 1942, although the deportation of Parisian Jews continued until 1944. This 1942 memo from Dannecker to Vichy police chief René Bousquet suggests ways of improving his quota:

'The recent operation for arresting stateless Jews in Paris has yielded only about 8000 adults and about 4000 children. But trains for the deportation of 40,000 Jews, for the moment, have been put in readiness by the Reich Ministry of Transport. Since the deportation of the children is not possible for the time being, the number of Jews ready for removal is quite insufficient. A further Jewish operation must therefore be started immediately. For this purpose Jews of Belgian and Dutch nationality may be taken into consideration, in addition to the former German, Austrian, Czech, Polish and Russian Jews who have so far been considered as being stateless. It must be expected, however, that this category will not yield sufficient numbers, and thus the French have no choice but to include those Jews who were naturalized in France after 1927, or even after 1919.' (Document from the trial of Adolf Eichmann, 1961.)

At the end of July, Eichmann instructed Dannecker to deport the children from Pithiviers and Beaune-la-Rolande; most of them were sent to Drancy. Here, they were packed 120 to a room, where they lay on a few dirty mattresses. These were quickly soiled from the diarrhoea caused by the cabbage soup being fed to the children; at night it was common for a whole room of 120 children to wake up as one and start crying together. After a few days, the children were deported to concentration camps and replaced with a new group: not one of them would return.

It is estimated that 9000 Parisians collaborated in Dannecker's Spring Wind, an atrocious crime that many say has never been adequately addressed by French society. In 1995, French President Jacques Chirac apologized for the role played by the Vichy government in the round-up; a plaque to its 8160 victims adorns a wall a few metres from where the demolished Vél' d'Hiv once stood.

ABOVE: Pithiviers was an internment camp for Parisian Jews en route to Nazi death camps such as Auschwitz. Novelist Irène Némirovsky was one of these internees.

The Fight Back

Even for those openly collaborating with the Germans, life under occupation was not easy. During the winter of 1940–41 there had been little to eat and the Nazis reduced the rations for each citizen to 1300 calories a day so they could keep their own cupboards filled. Ration cards were issued, but these did not guarantee food; shops were often empty. Some Parisians took to rearing pigeons and rabbits to survive the winter. Other everyday items would soon become luxury items from the past: shoe soles were crafted out of wood after leather supplies dwindled.

As time went on, it became clear that there would never be equality under the Reich. Paris and its citizens were simply another resource to be used up and

TIPS FOR THE OCCUPIED

Jean Texcier's *Conseils à l'Occupé* was a pamphlet of 33 tips for passive resistance against the Nazis, which was stuffed into letterboxes across the city. Although at a low, non-violent level, the tract was reported to provide a small light in the prevailing darkness:

• They are invaders. Be polite, but do not be friendly. Don't hurry to accommodate them. They will not reciprocate in the long run.
• If one of them addresses you in German, make a sign of confusion and move on. If he addresses you in French, you are not obliged to understand him.
• They march in your dishonour. Study a shop window instead of watching.
• If he asks you for a light, offer your cigarette. No one in human history has ever refused a light, even to the most traditional enemy.
• Show an elegant indifference but husband your anger, for you will need it. Be under no illusions: these men are not tourists.

(Jean Texcier, *Conseils à l'Occupé*, translated by Milton Dank)

discarded. It became clear that even non-Jewish Parisians were second-class citizens. A young engineer called Jacques Bonsergent became involved in a late-night scuffle with a German soldier. The city was shocked when Bonsergent was executed by firing squad on Christmas Eve at Fort Mont-Valérien. For many, defiance of the Reich began at that moment; women disobeyed orders and placed flowers beneath the posters announcing Bonsergent's execution. When these flowers were removed, more were laid in their place.

More direct action was to follow after Hitler declared war on the Soviet Union in 1941. In doing so he immediately lost the support of many pro-Russian French communists. Many of the young communists believed fervently in a future socialist state, and seemed unafraid of violent action to achieve it. Pierre Félix Georges was one such communist, who calmly shot Nazi officer Alfons Moser in the back as he waited for a train at the Barbès-Rochechouart metro station. The crowd enveloped Georges to protect him and allow him to escape. The fight back had begun.

Small resistance cells began operating around Paris, often in collaboration with Charles de Gaulle and the Free French Government in London. One of these 'Gaullist' cells, the Groupe du musée de l'Homme, was horrified by the general apathy and cowardice of Parisians towards the occupiers. In 1942, it published a famous newspaper, *Rèsistance*, calling on Parisians to stand up to the invaders. Other literature, including journalist Jean Texcier's *Conseils à l'Occupé*, or 'Tips For the Occupied' provided advice on how best to achieve this. However, members of the Vichy government infiltrated the Groupe du musée de l'Homme in 1942 and its members were executed. Operating under the watchful eye of the Reich and its collaborators was a desperately dangerous business.

As the war began to turn against Hitler in 1943, actions of resistance against the occupiers increased. Communist groups such as the Francs-Tireurs et Partisans (FTP) began a series of assassinations and sabotages against the Germans and Vichy government. After being defeated in his war against the Soviets, Hitler blamed the communists for everything, and his reprisals against those in Paris were swift and brutal. It is estimated that nearly 11,000 Parisian resistance fighters were executed during World War II, many of them at Fort Mont-Valérien, while a further were 5000 deported to the extermination camps.

As the likelihood of an Allied invasion of France grew, many collaborators switched sides. Some of these were even from the ranks of the despised Milice Française, the paramilitary group of the Vichy government formed to fight the Parisian resistance and coordinate Jewish deportations. The deportations would continue up until the liberation of Paris. With all available German manpower now being seconded to fight at the front, the 30,000-strong Milice were left to carry out their orders in Paris. Dressed in blue jackets and berets, the group gained a reputation for being better fascists than the Gestapo. But by 1944, their number was up: the liberation of the city began.

The Battle for Paris

The start of the insurrection against the Nazis came in the form of a police strike in August 1944. This was a cynical act by many policemen in order to save their own skins after the war. Other workers, however, also joined in, and soon there was fighting on the streets. In the time-honoured Parisian tradition, paving stones were pulled up and barricades built in the left-wing arrondissements of Belleville, Ménilmontant and Saint-Marcel. A spontaneous Parisian uprising had begun.

The Germans under the command of General Dietrich von Choltitz sent tanks and armoured cars to the city's hotpoints. Choltitz was in direct contact with Hitler, who, sinking further into madness, demanded that Paris should be

BELOW: Joseph Darnand, shown marching at the front, was a leader of the Vichy collaborators, creator of the Milice paramilitaries, and later, a German SS Officer. He was executed in 1945.

defended at all costs. If this could not be achieved, however, then the city would have to be destroyed. To carry out this order, Choltitz prepared demolition trucks filled with naval torpedoes and high explosives to be driven to the city's most treasured buildings. Hitler also offered to send a Karl-Gerät, the largest self-propelled gun ever made, which followed in the tradition of the Paris Gun of World War I. Built to fire a 2.5-tonne shell over 9.5km (6 miles) and used in the 1944 destruction of Warsaw, the Karl-Gerät was capable of destroying a whole building with one hit; fortunately, it would not fire a shot at Paris.

The Germans could not regain control of the city. Choltitz was desperately short of men to quell the uprising; his garrison of 16,000 was about the same size as the resistance forces, but the Nazis only had the weaponry and ammunition for a force a quarter of that size. Parisians now felt a blind hatred of the occupiers, and the violence against them proved to be contagious. Opportunistic fighters would show no signs of dissent while walking along the pavements, but would then draw revolvers and round up small groups of Germans when their backs were turned. Some threw Molotov cocktails under German cars, while others cheered them on from their balconies.

Soon tricolour flags were being flown from the tops of buildings on the Île de la Cité, which the resistance fighters had built into something of a fortress protected by barricades. Meanwhile, Charles de Gaulle was racing towards Paris after the Allied landing at Normandy. De Gaulle was terrified that Paris' communists would install a commune as soon as the Nazis had departed, something that was in the communists' minds also. De Gaulle had persuaded Dwight D. Eisenhower, the American general supervising the Allied invasion of Europe, to spare him the French Armoured Division to liberate Paris. Eisenhower

BELOW: The Battle of Paris began on 19 August 1944, when the French Resistance attacked the German soldiers left in the city. Nearly 1000 Resistance fighters died during the battle.

acquiesced, and also dispatched the US Fourth Division to help with the task.

Meanwhile, the German forces began their exodus from Paris, taking with them the main Parisian collaborators, including Pétain and other Vichy officials, and any last Parisian loot that was transportable. As the city fell, Hitler repeated his order that none of Paris' buildings should be left standing: 'The city must not fall into the enemy's hand except lying in complete rubble.' Hitler was said to have called Choltitz himself to make sure this had been down, screaming down the phone 'Is Paris burning?' A different account has Hitler asking the question of his chief of staff Alfred Jodl: 'Jodl, is Paris burning?' Choltitz himself later reported that he realized Hitler was insane and would not obey such an order. According to legend, Choltitz instead finished his lunch at the Hôtel Meurice, walked outside, and surrendered.

On 25 August, the French army under General Jacques-Philippe Leclerc entered Paris from the south. That Paris would be liberated by the French and not the Americans was a great political boon to de Gaulle: he would enter Paris as its saviour and new leader of the Provisional Government of the French Republic; there would be no communist commune. Paris, however, was in French hands once more.

ABOVE: Charles de Gaulle marches in liberated Paris with Resistance leader Georges Bidault (left). Bidault was twice elected Prime Minister, but later forced into exile for opposing de Gaulle's Algerian policy.

The Purge

Reprisals against Nazi collaborators began as soon as the city was liberated. Known as the épuration sauvage, or 'wild purge', the reprisals took the form of executions, public humiliations and assaults of suspected collaborators with a violent fervour not seen since the Terror of the 1790s. Spies, police informers, members of the Milice and the so-called collabos horizontales, women who had had sexual relations with the Nazis, were the first to be targeted.

Groups of Parisians rounded up these collabos horizontales before stripping and assaulting them and then shaving their heads. Sometimes the mob painted or branded swastikas on the women; at other times they would burn off all of their hair, tar and feather them, or find other ways to defile their bodies. One of the most famous Parisian collabos horizontales, known as Arletty, who spent the war living the life of high society among the Nazis, was dragged through the streets and reportedly had her breasts cut off. It is thought that up to 20,000 women were punished for their collaboration, although some numbers estimate that less than half of them actually played a collaborating role.

The collabos horizontales who had been shorn took to wearing turbans to hide their heads, which also became a signature of their crimes. In a horrible coincidence, the women returning to Paris from Ravensbrück and other

concentration camps also took to wearing turbans after having their heads shaved for lice. In another twist, the prostitutes who had serviced the brothels for Nazi officers were not shaved, after it was argued that they were just doing their jobs.

While the épuration sauvage was mostly unsanctioned violence carried out by mobs on the street, the épuration légale included trials against collaborators carried out in courts. Philippe Pétain was sentenced to death for treason in 1945 in one such court, later commuted to life imprisonment. Often, those awaiting trial were interned at Drancy and the Vélodrome d'Hiver. Between 1944 and 1951, 300,000 cases of collaboration were investigated and 6763 people were sentenced to death for treason and similar offences, although only 791 executions actually took place. The numbers executed under the épuration sauvage, by comparison, were thought to be around 10,000.

Many of the bodies of those killed were thrown into the Seine, where they floated to the surface and collected on its banks, just like the bodies of those sacrificed by the Parisii, the first masters of Paris. Many of the corpses were found tied to a limestone rock, with their hands bound behind their backs. In most cases the rock had not been heavy enough to sink the corpse. This method of execution was the notorious signature of the FTP, the communist party that was among the first to take up arms against the occupiers. The FTP held its own secret trials against collaborators in the basement of the Institut Dentaire George-Eastman, used as a Nazi hospital during the occupation. Other kangaroo courts were set up on street corners and the backs of parked trucks.

There can be no knowing how many innocents were killed during the purges, just as there is no way of knowing who was killed as the result of a rumour, grudge, or other score settling. At street level, no legal definition of collaboration was used in the trials of those accused. Paris became filled with paranoia: lists were drawn up and, like Robespierre's Great Terror, no one felt safe against a possible rap at their door. Many felt that they were still living under occupation.

Paris' Darkest Hour

In the end, the épurations brought no sense of closure to Paris: many felt sickened by the atrocities carried out in their name and guilty about those unjustly victimized. Others felt angry that so many who were clearly guilty were able to walk away unpunished, both Parisian collaborators and Nazis alike. Then, as newspaper reports and photographs showed the horrors that had taken place at extermination camps such as Auschwitz, Parisians were left to contemplate their complicity, inaction and indifference to the tens of thousands of Jewish citizens who had been rounded up and sent to their destruction. Paris had shown during the pre-war era that there was widespread and vehement xenophobia and anti-Semitism; now, at the end of the slaughter, it executed those who had aided the most virulent supporters of these ideologies. Perhaps this was Paris' darkest hour; it is arguably one that has been too easily forgotten.

OPPOSITE: The public shaming of the *collabos horizontales*, French women who had had sexual relations with the Germans. Others were stripped, branded, and tarred and feathered.

BELOW: Leader of the Vichy government and former war hero, Philippe Pétain was sentenced to death for his collaboration with the Nazis. He died in prison in 1951.

MODERN PARIS

Modern Paris was plagued by a new form of violence arising from France's colonial past. The struggle for independence in the French colonies led to battles on the streets of the capital. The Islamist violence of the twenty-first century, similarly, arose not just from distant conflicts, but from within the city's own embattled suburbs.

THE BLOODY HISTORY of Paris in the modern era arguably started with the May 1958 crisis, a planned coup d'état by French generals in Algiers. The military and various politicians believed that party politics were interfering with their suppression of rebels in the four-year Algerian War of Independence. Desperate to keep Algeria French, the generals ordered paratroopers from the French Algerian corps to seize Corsica and then mount a drop into Paris. Operation Resurrection would then take control of the government and demand the return of Charles de Gaulle. On 24 May, Corsica was won quickly and bloodlessly. Hearing this, the National Assembly immediately voted to bring de Gaulle back. The great hero of World War II was now expected to sort out the Algerian problem once and for all.

The war had started in 1954 when France was undergoing decolonization. It had not been a happy process. Under violent duress, France had let go of its colonial possessions in Indo-China, Morocco and Tunisia. Algeria, however, would not be easily abandoned. France had promised Algeria greater self-rule at

OPPOSITE: The Eiffel Tower lit in the red, white and blue of the tricolor following the 2015 terrorist attacks. Buildings around the world were similarly illuminated, including Tower Bridge and the Empire State Building.

This was the landscape that the 67-year-old Charles de Gaulle returned to in 1958. However, if the generals in Algiers had hoped for a green light for violent repression of the FLN in Algeria, they were wrong. In the end, de Gaulle would push for Algerian self-rule.

Uprisings in Modern Paris

The year of de Gaulle's resurrection saw an intensification of FLN violence in Paris. This was in response to the escalation of violence in Algeria itself, despite de Gaulle flying to Algiers and obscurely declaring to the Algerian people 'Je vous ai compris' ('I understand you') without actually ending French hostilities.

> **'Over the following weeks bloated corpses rose to the surface of the Seine.'**

In Paris, 7000 police had staged their own demonstrations in 1958 because they felt they did not have the power to put down the Algerian resistance. Egged on by far-right National Assembly member Jean-Marie Le Pen, 2000 of the demonstrators marched on the Assembly, chanting 'Mort aux fellaghas! A la Seine!' ('Death to the [Algerian] rebels! Into the Seine!'). Two months later, four policemen were killed in FLN bomb attacks. In response, Maurice Papon ordered the arrest of 5000 Algerians who were then detained in the former Vichy government internment centres for Jews, including the Vélodrome d'Hiver.

In 1961, the FLN killed 11 French policemen between August and October, leading Papon to announce a curfew between 8.30 p.m. and 5.30 a.m. for all 'Algerian Muslim workers', 'French Muslims' and 'French Muslims of Algeria'. This

A KING'S CONSTITUTION

De Gaulle had quit as French leader in a dramatic flourish in 1946, leaving the country in the hands of the Fourth Republic: an unstable series of 26 governments that came and went before de Gaulle's return. As a condition of his return, de Gaulle demanded emergency powers for six months and the introduction of a new presidential constitution giving him monarch-like powers. Under the constitution, the president would have the authority to dissolve the National Assembly, appeal to the French people directly by referendum, and to assume full powers. When a journalist accused de Gaulle of having the power to violate civil liberties, he retorted angrily:

'Have I ever done that? Quite the opposite, I have re-established them when they had disappeared. Who honestly believes that, at age 67, I would start a career as a dictator?'

Philosopher Jean-Paul Sartre, a vocal opponent of de Gaulle's and critic of the Algerian war, replied:

'When de Gaulle stated in all honesty that he would not take it into his head at the age of sixty-seven to impose a dictatorship he was left with a simple alternative: give up power, or become a dictator. For the situation determines the outcome… The solitude of this man enclosed within his own grandeur prevents him, whatever the circumstances, from becoming the leader of a republican state. Or, what comes down to the same thing, prevents the state of which he will be leader from remaining a Republic.'

was a farcical request, as the 150,000 Algerians living in Paris were considered French citizens and carried French identity cards. The FLN called on the entire Algerian population of Paris to march in protest. On 17 October 1961, between 30,000 and 40,000 unarmed Algerian men, women and children marched on the National Assembly. They were met by a level of police violence that horrified the rest of Paris. During the demonstration, Papon ordered his 10,000-strong police force to block all access points in and out of the city, and then arrested about 11,000 of the protesters. They were transported to various internment centres, beaten, and detained for several days without medical attention or food. Among the detained Algerians were Moroccans and Tunisians who had showed their solidarity by joining the march.

Meanwhile, a crowd of around 5000 protesters were blocked at the Pont de Neuilly by armed police who fired into the crowd and led charges with their *bidules* raised high. As the protest became a riot, police began throwing the protesters into the Seine, where many drowned.

After the riots ended, Papon instigated a police cover-up, and insisted that the police had only killed two Algerians during the violence. The others, he later told a court, had met their end at the hands of other Algerians. In 1998, a government commission found that 48 Algerians had been killed by the police; some claim that up to 200 died. Parisians, in any case, could see many had drowned: over the weeks following the so-called 'Battle for Paris', bloated corpses rose to the surface of the Seine and collected on its banks.

ABOVE: A protester gets caught up in police violence during a 1958 protest. Demonstrators ran the risk of serious injury or death at the hands of the police during this era.

There would be further violence. In February 1962, nine were killed during an FLN demonstration against the Organisation de l'Armée Secrète (OAS), a far-right paramilitary terror group trying to keep Algeria French. Once again, the deaths came at the hands of the police who charged the FLN and caused a crush at the Charonne metro station as thousands tried to take refuge inside. Then, in 1962, the Algerian War came to an end: the country was granted its independence by de Gaulle.

Immigrant Influx

The 1962 Évian Accords gave Algeria its independence and led to decolonization agreements across the French Empire. Under new repatriation laws, many immigrants were encouraged to move to France to fill the positions created by a booming economy.

There had been a general wave of immigration into Paris after World War II that included Italians, Germans, Russians and Portuguese, followed by ex-colonials from Indo-China, Tunisia, Morocco and West and North Africa. By the end of the twentieth century, foreigners made up around 13 per cent of Paris'

OPPOSITE: Thousands attend the 1962 funeral of the nine killed at the Charonne metro station. A crush had occurred when the police charged protesters down.

KILL DE GAULLE

The OAS were responsible for around 2000 deaths during its wave of terror between 1954 and 1962. Among its high-profile targets were Jean-Paul Sartre, a supporter of the FLN, and Charles de Gaulle. The most prominent would-be assassin of de Gaulle was Jean Bastien-Thiry, a former lieutenant-colonel of the air force. On 22 August 1962, Bastien-Thiry and a group of gunmen sprayed de Gaulle's car with machine-gun bullets as he drove through the suburb of Petit-Clamart. Miraculously, de Gaulle, his wife, and a chicken in the boot all survived the ordeal: although 14 bullets penetrated the Citroën DS and two of its tyres were shot out, it was still able to speed away. The trial of Bastien-Thiry, the last man to be executed by firing squad in France, concluded that the assassination attempt had failed because the terrorists had been 'bad shots': more than 200 spent shell casings had been

ABOVE: Protesters march against the far-right OAS, the group responsible for the assassination attempt on de Gaulle.

found on the pavement around the crime scene. The episode was later fictionalized in Frederick Forsyth's 1971 book *The Day of the Jackal*.

population and many arrondissements took on their own cultural identities. The 13th arrondissement became known as Chinatown, with a large Vietnamese and Cambodian population; many Turks settled in the 9th arrondissement; Jews settled in the Marais district of the 3rd and 4th arrondissements; North Africans took up residence in the 18th, 19th and 20th arrondissements and their various outlying banlieues; hundreds of mosques were also built.

Housing, however, had not kept up. By the 1950s, virtually no housing had been built in Paris for 25 years. Eighty per cent of Parisian apartments did not have a bathroom and 55 per cent did not have a toilet. Many immigrants were forced to live in shantytowns called *bidonvilles* made from cardboard, plywood

REVOLUTIONARY GRAFFITI

During the May protests, students painted Paris with revolutionary slogans. Some of these had been borrowed from previous revolutions, but now reached a far greater audience thanks to the television news. The hundreds of slogans showed a widespread dissatisfaction with society, but stopped short of a focused attempt to bring about change. Instead, the protesters, like those of the 1870 Commune, wanted a revolutionary overhaul of society. This is what worried de Gaulle. Some of the slogans read:

BELOW: The 1968 graffiti reads 'Be realistic, demand the impossible!'

- 'Be realistic, demand the impossible!'
- 'Beneath the paving stones – the beach!'
- 'When the National Assembly becomes a bourgeois theatre, all the bourgeois theatres should be turned into national assemblies.'
- 'All power corrupts. Absolute power corrupts absolutely.'
- 'Professors, you are as senile as your culture, your modernism is nothing but the modernization of the police.'
- 'Barricades close the streets but open the way.'
- 'Humanity won't be happy till the last capitalist is hung with the guts of the last bureaucrat.'
- 'I'm a Groucho Marxist.'
- 'How can you think freely in the shadow of a chapel?'

and corrugated iron. In response, the government built a series of large low-income housing projects in the banlieues. Often built far from markets and public transport with few amenities and shops, these soon became the domain of North African immigrants.

Increased immigration in the 1960s, combined with the baby boom of the 1950s, sparked a growth boom in the banlieues. However, in the 1970s there was a downturn – deindustrialization in Paris led to widespread unemployment. From that point on, the banlieue housing projects became notorious as poverty traps for immigrants and their offspring. In the 1980s, youths born in the banlieues to North African immigrants came of age. Railing against discrimination by the police and the endless cycle of poverty and despair, the *banlieusards* began burning cars, attacking police and causing general unrest in their neighbourhoods. It was a situation that intensified towards the end of the century.

May 1968

The 30 years of economic prosperity, or *Trente Glorieuses*, that had led many immigrants to Paris in the 1960s had also led to the building of a new city university, Nanterre. Although labelled a 'model university', Nanterre was in fact made up of a drab, gray campus in the outlying suburbs. The long commute from central Paris was only one problem faced by its mainly white middle-class

ABOVE: The rise of the *bidonville* shanty towns in the 1950s led directly to the government's low-income housing projects in the banlieues.

ABOVE: Students engage the police in running battles on the streets of Paris, May, 1968. Satellite broadcasting allowed images of the protests to be instantly beamed around the world.

students; the university was also overcrowded and run according to outdated conservative traditions.

Railing against all of this, students staged a sudden occupation of the main Nanterre building on 22 March 1968. Invoking the revolutionary spirit of 1789, 1848 and 1870, the students demanded an overhaul of the education system. In response, the university shut down. Students of the Sorbonne in Paris' Latin Quarter then picked up the revolutionary mantle and organized a march to protest against the Nanterre closure. Staged for 3 May, this was met with a heavily armed police response. As more than 200,000 students marched on the buildings of the Sorbonne they were charged by the CRS riot police wielding batons; barricades were then quickly thrown up and a running battle ensued. The violence ended with the police taking over the Sorbonne campus.

It was only the second time in its 700-year history that the university had been closed; the first had been during the Nazi occupation. Symbolically, it was a blow for de Gaulle, who was celebrating 10 years in power. Worse was to follow for the president, as the protests became larger, more violent, and eventually threatened to bring the government to its knees. Meanwhile, the world's media watched on. Satellite broadcasts allowed images of the demonstrations to be beamed instantly across the world – as had those of similar student protests in 1968 in Warsaw, Rome, London and America.

10 May was another flashpoint, when a large crowd congregated on the Rive Gauche. When the CRS blocked the protesters' route the demonstration became a riot: paving stones were duly ripped up to make barricades; Molotov cocktails were thrown at the police; cars were overturned and set on fire; shop windows were smashed; bus tyres slashed and cars overturned. During the destruction, Red Cross workers in helmets ducked under clouds of teargas to give first aid to hundreds of casualties. Television images of students covered with blood were broadcast to shocked worldwide audiences as police clubbed protesters armed with paving stones.

With hundreds of protesters now in jail, another march was organized for 13 May to call for their release. The government tried to placate the protesters by announcing the release of the prisoners and the reopening of the Sorbonne. However, this did not stop the protests, and now workers had joined the cause. By 20 May, more than 10 million French workers, around two-thirds of the French workforce, went out on strike. Among the workers' demands were higher wages, better working conditions, and the ousting of Charles de Gaulle as president. De Gaulle responded by warning that France faced civil war and was 'on the brink of paralysis'. Meanwhile, protesters stormed the Paris Stock Exchange and set it alight. Some hours later, after the fire had been put out, it emerged that de Gaulle had fled the country for Germany.

De Gaulle knew that his last line of defence was the army. He had fled to the Rhine to ask the French military leaders based there whether he had their support.

BELOW: Members of the trade union Confédération générale du travail (CGT) come out on strike in 1968. It turned into the largest general strike in French history.

With this confirmed, de Gaulle made an announcement on French radio that he would dissolve the country's National Assembly and call a snap election on 23 June. He also ordered all striking workers to return to work or he would declare a state of emergency. Rumours soon reached the protesters that army tanks were rolling towards Paris.

In the end, a counter-revolutionary protest saved de Gaulle when 800,000 of his supporters marched down the Champs-Élysées waving the tricolour. So it was that May 1968 became the revolution that never was. The strikers returned to work and the students went back to university. De Gaulle won the election of 23 June by the greatest margin in French electoral history. However, it was his last hurrah; he died the following year.

The New Terror

In the 1980s, Islamic terrorists launched a new campaign in Paris. These included a grenade attack on the Jewish Goldberg restaurant in 1982 and a bombing on a train between Paris and Marseille in 1983. In 1986 there were several more bombings including at a Champs-Élysées shopping centre, the Hôtel de Ville, the headquarters of Renault cars, and the Tati department store, where seven people were killed.

The attacks escalated in 1995: on 25 July a bomb exploded at the Saint-Michel metro station killing eight people and wounding 80; on 6 October, a gas bottle bomb injured 13 at the Maison Blanche metro station. Then, on 3 December 1996, four people died when a bomb exploded at the Gare de Port-Royal. Behind

BELOW: Counter-revolutionaries wave the tricolor as they march down the Champs-Élysées in support of de Gaulle. He would win the following election in a landslide victory.

SIXTIES GOODBYE

As the last promise of a revolution in Paris died with the election of de Gaulle, the death of the 1960s counter-culture came with the demise of its American pop heroes: Janis Joplin, Jimi Hendrix and Jim Morrison. Morrison lived out his last days in Paris, where he hoped to leave rock stardom behind for a career as a poet. He famously died in the bath on 3 July 1971, in his Rue Beautreillis apartment, probably from a heroin overdose. No one can be sure, however, as no autopsy was performed; three years later, his partner, Pamela Courson, the only other person in the apartment at the time, also died of an overdose. Morrison was buried in the Père Lachaise Cemetery, where his grave remains one of the most visited tourist attractions in Paris.

RIGHT: Jim Morrison's grave at the Père Lachaise Cemetery remains popular and well tended.

the attacks were Algerian Islamists, the Groupe Islamique Armé (GIA), aiming to bring great terror to the city during the climax of the Algerian civil war taking place at the time. The GIA wished to install an Islamic state in place of the Algerian government, which it blamed the French government for supporting. Its leader, Khaled Kelkal, was hunted down by French police and shot after the Gare de Port-Royal bombing.

The attacks added to the strains between Paris and its Algerian immigrants. The 1990s were a dark period in Parisian race relations, with the right-wing National Front making great gains in popularity, including among many of the North African banlieues that other Parisians believed responsible for the recent terrorism.

A telling moment in race relations occurred in 1998, when the French football team unexpectedly defeated the Brazilians in the World Cup final played at the Stade de France. The French captain, Zinedine 'Zizou' Zidane, became an instant sensation; his image was projected onto the Arc de Triomphe underneath the words 'Merci Zizou'. A million Parisians of all classes broke onto the streets in spontaneous celebration of the win, staying up to belt out the 'Marseillaise' throughout the night and drown themselves in champagne. However, Zidane himself was of Algerian origin brought up in the banlieues of Marseille. After the decade often described by the media as the *malaise française*, the 'Effet Zidane' was hailed as the start of a new cultural era of tolerance in France. The national football team could champion this new fraternity, as many of the 'Rainbow team'

ABOVE: Police cordon off the area after the 1982 terrorist attack on Paris' Goldberg restaurant.

were descended from immigrants: Youri Djorkaeff was Armenian; Lilian Thurum was from Guadeloupe; Patrick Vieira from Senegal; and Zidane, Algerian. It was enough for National Front leader Jean-Marie Le Pen to describe the French football team as 'artificial' because it was made up of too few white Gauls.

However, the idea of racial and colonial reconciliation through football soured when the French team played Algeria shortly after the 9/11 attacks on America. The match was mired in violence from the outset and Zidane and other French players were accused of being traitors to the Islamic cause. The Algerian fans shouted 'long live Osama bin Laden' from the stands and then invaded the pitch 15 minutes before the final whistle. Jean-Marie Le Pen won 17 per cent of the vote for the presidential elections later that year.

Worse was to come. Several nights of rioting broke out in 2005 in the banlieue of Clichy-sous-Bois, an area with a high population of Algerians. Groups of youths set cars alight, threw missiles and took part in running battles with police after two teenagers were electrocuted while hiding from police in a power substation. The frayed relationship between inhabitants of the banlieue and the state were further exacerbated when Interior Minister Nicolas Sarkozy was pelted with stones and bottles while visiting the scene. Sarkozy suggested to the residents of Clichy-sous-Bois that the crime-ridden banlieues be 'cleaned out with a power hose' and called the 'rabble' responsible for the riots 'gangrene' and 'scum'.

Sarkozy sent reinforcements from the CRS to quell the continuing riots, but they spread to other banlieues around Paris, including Grigny in the city's south. After 14 nights of consecutive violence the rioting calmed, and then died out. Two had been killed, 2888 people arrested, and €200 million of damage done. In his first speech since the rioting began, President Jacques Chirac promised to overhaul the banlieues and provide new opportunities for its young people. In 2016, however, residents of the Paris banlieues told visiting journalists that little had changed.

> **'After 14 nights of consecutive violence the rioting calmed, and then died out.'**

A City at War

In 2015, Paris was struck by the two worst terror attacks of the modern era. In January, three gunmen slaughtered the editorial staff of satirical magazine *Charlie Hebdo* and shoppers inside a kosher supermarket. In November, a coordinated series of attacks were carried out across the city by nine terrorists who, armed with grenades, Kalashnikov assault rifles, and explosive suicide belts, killed 130

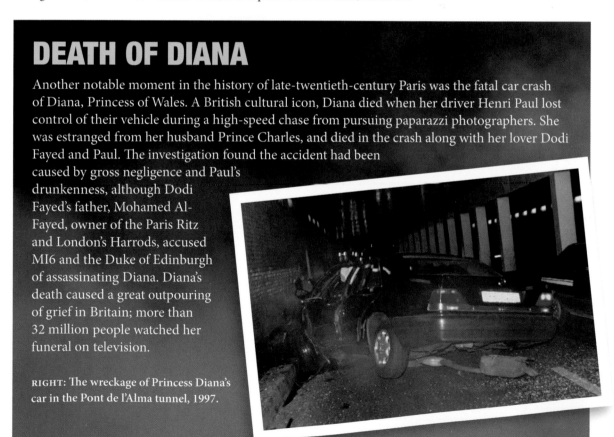

DEATH OF DIANA

Another notable moment in the history of late-twentieth-century Paris was the fatal car crash of Diana, Princess of Wales. A British cultural icon, Diana died when her driver Henri Paul lost control of their vehicle during a high-speed chase from pursuing paparazzi photographers. She was estranged from her husband Prince Charles, and died in the crash along with her lover Dodi Fayed and Paul. The investigation found the accident had been caused by gross negligence and Paul's drunkenness, although Dodi Fayed's father, Mohamed Al-Fayed, owner of the Paris Ritz and London's Harrods, accused MI6 and the Duke of Edinburgh of assassinating Diana. Diana's death caused a great outpouring of grief in Britain; more than 32 million people watched her funeral on television.

RIGHT: The wreckage of Princess Diana's car in the Pont de l'Alma tunnel, 1997.

people at cafés, restaurants and the Bataclan concert theatre. French President François Hollande declared a state of emergency after the attacks, saying 'France is at war'. The attacks raised many questions about the role of homegrown Islamic extremism in Paris and the radicalization of its disenfranchised youths.

Saïd and Chérif Kouachi, brothers of Algerian descent brought up in the 19th arrondissement, attacked *Charlie Hebdo* for its controversial cartoons of the prophet Muhammad; some considered the satirical cartoons a blasphemy punishable by death. Radicalized by a guru from a local mosque, the brothers were jailed after trying to join a Jihadist group in Syria. In Fleury-Mérogis Prison, the brothers met their future accomplice Amedy Coulibaly, a second-generation Mali immigrant from the Grigny banlieue, and Djamel Beghal, an international terrorist who mentored the group. In 2011, Saïd Kouachi trained with terrorist group al-Qaeda in the Arabian Peninsula, who helped him buy Kalashnikovs and a rocket-propelled grenade launcher in Paris through contacts in the Belgian underworld.

On 7 January 2015, the Kouachi brothers forced their way into the offices of *Charlie Hebdo* and executed 11 members of its staff who were having a morning editorial meeting. Identifying themselves as members of Al-Qaeda in Yemen and shouting 'We have avenged the Prophet Muhammad, we have killed *Charlie Hebdo*!' the brothers made their escape in a getaway car after shooting a policeman outside. Two days later the brothers were found at a printworks on the

BELOW: **Protesters call for respect, justice and religious tolerance during a fifth night of violence in the Clichy-sous-Bois banlieue.**

edge of Paris, where they had taken a hostage. A police siege ended in a hail of bullets as the brothers ran out of the building. Meanwhile, a similar siege took place at a kosher supermarket at Porte de Vincennes, where the third terrorist, Amedy Coulibaly, had also taken hostages and killed four.

Friday 13 November

Ten months later there occurred a still greater atrocity. In the evening of Friday 13 November, three teams of terrorists began a coordinated and systematic attack across Paris. At 9.20 p.m., the first group targeted the Stade de France, where a football match between Germany and France was being played. Among the 80,00 spectators were François Hollande and German chancellor Angela Merkel, but the three terrorists armed with explosive suicide belts could not get inside the stadium and instead detonated their belts outside, killing one spectator. Minutes later across town in the 11th arrondissement, gunmen in a black vehicle began shooting café and restaurant patrons sitting outside. Thirty-nine people were killed and 28 people were wounded in these attacks, which included the detonation of an explosive belt identical to those used at the Stade de France.

At 9.40 p.m., three terrorists entered the Bataclan, a 1500-person concert theatre where a sold-out performance by the band the Eagles of Death Metal was being held. With shouts of 'Allahu akbar', the gunmen fanned out around the hall and fired on the crowd, throwing grenades and shooting people indiscriminately. Some survivors managed to escape out of two emergency exits, and by climbing onto the roof and hiding in the building's toilets and offices.

After 20 minutes of shooting the terrorists collected around 100 hostages as armed police gathered outside. One of them was heard to yell in French, 'This is because of all the harm done by Hollande to Muslims all over the world.' The Islamic State (ISIS) later claimed responsibility for the attacks, saying it was in response to French airstrikes on ISIS targets in Syria and Iraq. At 12.20 a.m., a tactical unit from the Brigades de Recherche et d'Intervention (BRI) stormed the building. The full-length metal shield they used during the assault was found to have been shot 27 times. The police later described that they believed they were walking in water when they entered the building, but this turned out to be blood. Within three minutes the gunmen were dead, one of them by detonating his explosive belts; they had taken 89 lives. The attack was over.

ABOVE: Police and forensic teams cordon off the street below the *Charlie Hebdo* offices. Here, the terrorists shot at police before making their escape in a black Citroen.

INSIDE THE BATACLAN

This eyewitness account of the Bataclan shooting came from Julien Pierce, a *Europe 1* radio journalist who was inside the theatre:

'Two or three men, without masks, came in with Kalashnikov-type automatic weapons and began shooting blindly at the crowd... it lasted 10, 15 minutes. It was extremely violent and there was a wave of panic. Everyone was running in all directions towards the stage. It was a stampede and even I was trampled. I saw a lot of people hit by bullets. The gunmen had loads of time to reload at least three times. They weren't masked, they knew what they were doing, they were very young. There were bodies everywhere. It was a bloodbath.'

LEFT: Eagles of Death Metal members Jesse Hughes and Dave Catching visit the memorial to the Bataclan concert victims.

Into the Future

Before he was shot during the police stand-off in the kosher supermarket, terrorist Amedy Coulibaly calmly made himself a sandwich and told a hostage: 'I was born in France... if they hadn't attacked Muslims abroad I wouldn't be here. I'm telling you just so you know what's going on. There will be many more like me, many more will come.'

His words had a horrible resonance. Ten months later, France was once again under attack. On 14 July 2016, the day François Hollande was to announce the lifting of the state of emergency imposed in November, an ISIS attack was launched against the city of Nice. During the attack 84 were killed when an extremist drove a truck into a crowd at a Bastille Day fireworks display. Then, only 12 days later, two teenagers claiming allegiance to ISIS stormed a Normandy church and slit the throat of an 85-year-old priest.

It was the first time the Church had been targeted in an Islamist attack in France, and many centuries since blood had been spilled on consecrated ground. Centuries before, the violence between Catholics and Protestants in the Wars of Religion had eventually led to the secularist policy now so important to France. The separation of the Church from the state was officially sealed in 1905 when Catholic fervour was high and the Assumptionist newspaper *La Croix* promoted the French 'race', in opposition to the republican notion that humanity is made up of all people.

In the modern era, the state's policy of secularism, known as *laïcité*, was behind the 2004 banning of Muslim headscarves in schools and the 2010 general ban on face covering – a law that forbids the wearing of the Muslim niqab and the burqa. The state follows *laïcité* obsessively, believing it to bridge all gaps, creating universalism between people regardless of religion. Others argue that the banning of headscarves instead singles out Muslims and inflames sectarian hatred.

It was in the name of secularism that the cartoonists at *Charlie Hebdo* exercised their legal right to mock the Prophet Muhammad. Thousands in Paris and around the world then championed the slogan 'Je suis Charlie', or 'I am Charlie' to show their solidarity after the 2015 attacks; many in the media described it as a rallying cry for freedom of self-expression. Others suggested it was not an expression of positive French values, but a way of rallying right wing-elements that blamed immigration for the attacks. Some even suggested that by being deliberately provocative and showing caricatures of Arabs, the cartoons of *Charlie Hebdo* were feeding into the culture of hate also propagated by the right.

The right is certainly quick to exploit cultural and religious divisions. Marine Le Pen, who became leader of the National Front after sacking her father Jean-Marie Le Pen for being too anti-Semitic, gained much popular support following the November attacks. 'The influx of migrants must be stopped,' said Le Pen, arguing that French identity is undermined by Muslim culture. Many from the left were aghast that cries of anti-immigrant hatred, which has plagued the history of Paris for so many centuries, could drown out the republican notions of tolerance and fraternity.

BELOW: **The truck used by a terrorist in Nice to run down pedestrians following a Bastille Day fireworks display. Bullet holes in the windscreen show where police tried to stop the driver.**

The *Charlie Hebdo* massacre triggered an outpouring of grief in Paris. 'Je Suis Charlie' became the slogan of solidarity used around the world.

The anti-immigration argument, moreover, tends to overlook the fact that many who carry out terrorist attacks are actually French citizens. The *Charlie Hebdo* attackers, called by Parisian newspaper *Libération* 'kids of France', were second-generation immigrants born in Paris who lived on the margins of society. The lawyer who defended the Kouachi brothers called them 'lost children of the Republic' who had been radicalized in the Paris banlieues. Chérif Kouachi described himself as a 'Ghetto Muslim': he was brought up in care homes, had little education and worked in dead-end jobs. Those children and grandchildren of the banlieues often describe themselves as not feeling French and being left without a future. Many feel they are fighting the same battles fought by their parents and grandparents when they first settled in France.

At that time, immigrants from French colonies such as Algeria were invited to Paris to fill labour shortages. Then when the jobs disappeared they felt abandoned in the banlieues, on the fringes both symbolically and geographically. After the *Charlie Hebdo* attacks the threat from within became clear: terrorism no longer had a front line. Algerians carrying French passports have committed slaughter in the offices of liberal Paris; now, for those on the right, all French

'The killers were often born and bred in the slums of Paris.'

BELOW: The popularity of National Front leader Marine le Pen rose following the 2015 terror attacks. Le Pen blamed the atrocities on immigration and Islam.

Muslims are a threat. The danger to the values of the Republic seemed clear enough: this was cold-blooded murder in the name of Jihad, where an elderly priest could be slaughtered on his own altar. Some took this as a renewal of traditional wars of religion against Islam, and called for a new crusade in retaliation. But the killing did not come out of nowhere. The killers were often born and bred in the slums of Paris; they were part of France and they were the enemies of France; they wanted revenge for ancient colonial wrongs and for ultra-modern Western wars carried out in their Middle Eastern homelands; some said they wanted an Islamist state, but many were obvious casualties of France's failure to create an inclusive society.

ABOVE: A memorial for the priest Jacques Hamel killed by terrorists in the church of Saint-Etienne du Rouvray, Normandy. The ID card of 19-year-old terrorist Abdel Malik Petitjean shows he was a French citizen.

History Marches On

Paris, of course, has seen repeated insurrections and riots during its long history. To the great Parisian struggles – between the left and right, between monarchs and subjects, Catholics and Protestants, inhabitants and invaders, and the state and its citizens – is now added the seething contradictions of Islamism and immigrant resentment. Here is a new form of terror quite unlike the revolutionary Terror of the 1790s, and presenting possibly an even greater challenge to the existing order. Paris explodes in fire and hate: can the City of Light resist the terror without sacrificing its ideals of liberty, equality and fraternity?

BIBLIOGRAPHY

Andress, David, *The Terror: Civil War in the French Revolution* (Little, Brown, 2005)

Barclay, Steven (Ed.), *A Place in the World Called Paris* (Chronicle Books, 2004)

Baxter, Jon, *Paris at the End of the World* (Harper Perennial, 2014)

Bernier, Olivier, *Fireworks at Dusk: Paris in the Thirties* (Little, Brown, 1993)

Braudel, F., *The Identity of France* (Collins, 1988)

Bull, Marcus (Ed.) *France in the Central Middle Ages* (OUP, 2003)

Collins, James, *The State in Early Modern France* (Cambridge University Press, 2009)

Cobban, A., *A History of Modern France* (Pelican, 1970)

Cooper, Artemis; Beevor, Antony, *Paris: After The Liberation 1944-1949* (Penguin, 2004)

Doyle, William, *The Oxford History of the French Revolution* (OUP, 1989)

Drake, David, *Paris at War 1939-1944* (Harvard University Press, 2015)

Duby, Georges, *France in the Middle Ages, 987-1460: From Hugh Capet to Joan of Arc* (Blackwell, 1991)

Drinkwater, J. F., *Roman Gaul: The Three Provinces* (Croom Helm, 1983)

Fraser, Antonia, *Love and Louis XIV: The Women in the Life of the Sun King* (W&N, 2007)

Goubert, Pierre, *The Course of French History* (Routledge, 1988)

Hobsbawm, Eric, *The Age of Revolution: Europe, 1789-1848* (Abacus, 1988)

Horne, Alistair, *Seven Ages of Paris* (Pan Books, 2002)

Hunt, Lynn, *Politics, Culture, and Class in the French Revolution* (University of California Press, 2004)

Hussey, Andrew, *Paris: The Secret History* (Penguin, 2007)

James, Edward, *The Origins of France: Clovis to the Capetians 500-1000* (Palgrave Macmillan, 1982)

Jenkins, Cecil, *A Brief History of France: People, History and Culture* (Robinson, 2011)

Jones, Colin, *Paris: Biography of a City* (Penguin, 2006)

Jones, Colin, *The Great Nation* (Penguin, 2002)

Knecht, R. J., *The French Wars of Religion 1559-1598* (Longman, 1996)

McAuliffe, Mary, *Dawn of the Belle Epoque* (Rowan & Littlefield, 2011)

Piggott, Stuart (Ed.) *France Before the Romans* (Thames and Hudson, 1974)

Price, Roger, *A Concise History of France* (Cambridge University Press, 1993)

Price, Roger, *A Social History of Nineteenth-Century France* (Hutchinson, 1987)

Roberts, Andrew, *Napoleon the Great* (Penguin, 2015)

Robert, Cole, *A Traveller's History of Paris* (Cassell, 1994)

Roche, Daniel, France in the Enlightenment, (Harvard University Press, 1992)

Rosbottom, Ronald C., *When Paris Went Dark* (Back Bay Books, 2015)

Roux, Simone, *Paris in the Middle Ages* (PENN, 2003)

Russell, John, *Paris* (B T Batsford Ltd, 1960)

Schama, Simon, *Citizens: A Chronicle of the French Revolution* (Viking, 1989)

Sutherland, D., *France, 1789-1815: Revolution and Counterrevolution* (Harpercollins, 1985)

Tocqueville, Alexis de, *The Old Regime and the French Revolution* (Doubleday, 1995)

Todd, E., The Making of Modern France (Blackwell, 1991)

Tombs, Robert, *France 1814-1914* (Longman, 1996)

Wright, D. G., Napoleon and Europe (Routledge, 1985)

Zeldin, Theodore, *France 1848-1945: Taste and Corruption* (OUP, 1980)

INDEX

PICTURE CREDITS

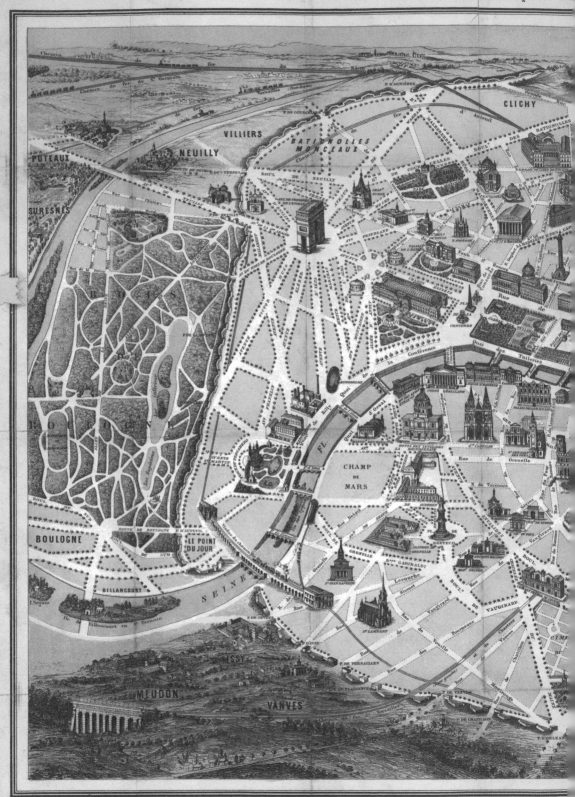

Gravé par F. DUFOUR.

GARNIER FRÈRES